TAKING THE LONG WAY HOME

Soul Searching Across America

Sonja Millings

DEDICATION

This book is lovingly dedicated to my husband, Howard (aka Mr. Wonderful), who has never met a detour he could resist. I love you to the moon and back, and cannot imagine my life without you.

CONTENTS

INTRODUCTION

I fell in love with a man who loves to travel. Many years after our first date, while in the middle of Iowa on a lonely stretch of highway with nothing but corn fields as far as the eye could see, I had an epiphany: I married Huck Finn.

During our courtship, he took me on amazing vacations to Europe, as well as quick getaways to quirky places like Clear Lake, Iowa, for a concert honoring the 50th anniversary of Buddy Holly's death. Before we got married in 2010, the two of us would spontaneously jump in the car on a lazy Sunday afternoon, without a destination in mind, and come home with great stories about touring Forest Lawn Cemetery, or riding the high-speed ferry to Catalina Island.

From the time we first met on match.com in 2006, to the present, every month has been full of new stories. He has more of a sense of adventure than anyone I've ever met. Early on, I realized that as long as we were together, my life would never be boring.

My work required weekly travel throughout the United States. To me, travel meant rushing through busy airports; losing my patience with people who couldn't navigate their way through security without holding up the line; changing time zones without bothering to unpack in hotel rooms; meetings and conferences; ride-alongs with sales reps; and dinner with clients. The Starbucks crew at the John Wayne Airport smiled when they saw me in line and greeted me by name. I flew so often that the airline sent me a hand-signed birthday card before it was a marketing strategy. I often found myself discussing the merits of support hose (to prevent blood clots) with flight attendants.

In spite of my longing for stability, I rarely minded when Howard began spending a lot of time researching online for our next adventure. A day or weekend with Mr. Wonderful at the wheel was pure bliss. A week or ten days in Europe—even more bliss. It was simply impossible not to have a good time with him.

Surely, a yearlong road trip would just be more of the same, right?

Wrong.

I could not have predicted how our differences would amplify at the worst possible times.

Four years after we met, he proposed to me on Valentine's Day on a beach in Carmel, California. We were married in a small ceremony a month later. Like most couples, we'd had many conversations about lifelong dreams; mine involved a little place near the sea with room for a garden, and his was to roam the country for a year with little or no itinerary.

We both retired in late January of 2012. Two weeks later, on February 15, we set off on a yearlong adventure in a 22' RV with our 11-year-old Golden Retriever, Emily. My other Golden, Molly, had died four years earlier. Emily, Molly and I, had been a tight little pack of three until Howard came into our lives, but it didn't take long for them to accept him as the new dog in our pack after he not-so-secretly snuck food to them under the table, and happily complied with their constant demands for attention and affection. After Molly died, "my" dog Emily became "our" dog Emily.

Prior to the trip, and in spite of almost six years as a couple, *we had never spent more than two consecutive weeks together.* Time apart had always given us something to talk about when we saw each other again. Regular chunks of solitude were required to re-charge our marital batteries and put petty grievances in perspective. I wondered—could we be good sports when things got rough, or would we end up divorced from too much togetherness? Would ever-changing scenery and long hours of being still help or hurt my adult ADHD? In the past, I'd been able to hide from the painful parts of my life. Was I ready to confront my demons in the midst of all that stillness?

The biggest elephant in the room was impossible to fathom at the time and required the most courage: what would remain when the things I'd worked so hard to acquire throughout my adult life—mostly my own house and lucrative career—were gone?

What would be left of *me* after subtracting those things?

As I contemplated the future without a paycheck, I felt the room grow smaller. Where were the books to help me with those questions?

Writing has always been a form of therapy for me. In addition to an online travel blog, on which we took turns posting our observations, I also kept a personal journal. The blog was the nuts and bolts of the trip ("today we visited …") while my journal held what I jokingly referred to as the real story.

This is *our* real story. Oh, sure—there's a fair share of sunshine and jazz hands, but there's also the other side of the story about the long days of silence, enduring bone-jarring potholes on interstate highways, and arguing about whose turn it was to select music on the satellite radio. The petty stuff was easy; the hard part was documenting what happened when I eliminated the noise and distractions of my busy life and untethered my soul for the first time.

This is the book I was looking for before we left on our trip.

CHAPTER 1
PRE-TRIP ANXIETY

We had been fighting almost non-stop for months. Retirement was looming. I was in agony over getting rid of most of my belongings in yet another garage sale. I cannot tell you how much I hated bickering over 50-cent items. Howard loved garage sales—especially the negotiations. I had to bite my tongue when he gave away my relatively new circular saw for $7. The worst part was watching my memories tied to the roof of a stranger's car and slowly disappearing down the road. When a cranky woman with three very tired kids in tow balked at the price of my distressed and much-loved bedroom set, I lost it.

"Three hundred dollars?" she barked.

"That's a bargain! You're getting a Pottery Barn queen-size bed frame, headboard, footboard, side panels, and two matching end tables!" I barked right back at her.

"It looks scraped-up," she said, without blinking.

"It's supposed to look that way—it's distressed!" I wanted to slap her.

Howard appeared out of nowhere and offered to drop the price to $199. Before I could open my mouth, the woman sniffed, curled her lip, and said, "I'll give you $50—take it or leave it." I asked her to leave. Once she was gone, I grabbed my car keys and left my husband to deal with the rest of the garage sale without me.

My head was constantly fighting with my heart. Howard was much more pragmatic. We agreed that we had to downsize to reduce the number of things in storage for a year, but Howard had very few emotional connections to his belongings. He didn't understand why the dark green wrought iron patio furniture, or the lion-head wall fountain, was so important to me. I told him how I'd found the patio furniture on sale at a time when I couldn't afford it at the regular price. As for the fountain, it was also for my first house. I had to drag it into the back yard on a blanket because I had no one to help me get it back there. I was a raw nerve when it came to making decisions about what to keep and what to get rid of, because I wanted to keep everything. Every chair, rug, and picture on the wall, held deep emotional connections to the home I'd created ten years prior to meeting my husband.

A house had always symbolized security, love, and connection—especially when I was a single parent. When I was a kid, I used to ride my bike around the block when my parents argued, stopping to stare at my favorite houses, and pretending that I lived in one of them with a much happier family. I also remember walking to school in the second grade, noticing which houses needed a rocking chair and a big glazed pot of red flowers on the porch; or a new coat of paint and some white glossy shutters; perhaps a big tree in the front yard with a rope swing. I thought if I could just find the right house, a sense of belonging would follow.

I worked my way up the ladder of a global corporation, which enabled me to buy my first home in Sacramento, California, in 1998. I saved for the down payment, stayed within my budget, and paid for the furnishings with cash instead of going on vacations. After 10 years of living in apartments as a single parent with my young daughter, I was finally able to give her a real home with a backyard and not one, but two, Golden Retriever puppies.

I bought comfortable furniture and a sturdy kitchen table around which my friends and family would gather. Little by little, I turned it into my dream home.

Thirteen years later, it was being dismantled one garage sale at a time, as I stood by and watched.

CHAPTER 2
MEETING MR. WONDERFUL

We met on match.com in 2006. He was "Traveling Man Frank" and I was "Hopeful Romantic." It had been a year since I'd relocated to Thousand Oaks—a beautiful upscale city in Southern California, 12 miles from the beach in Malibu—for a new job. Thousand Oaks was surrounded by protected greenbelts and rolling hills. My new job was a 10-minute commute and, although I bought at the height of the housing bubble (choosing from a narrow field of options), I was happy in my new townhouse. It was a lot more than I'd planned to spend, but the bubble worked both ways and I had money from the sale of my home in Sacramento for a 20% down payment on my new place.

Watching the lights of the city at night from my living room balcony, or walking the dogs in the nearby botanical garden, settled the recurring sense of homelessness I'd felt for most of my life. Our daily walks slowed down my thoughts, and it wasn't long before I found a comfortable rhythm to my days. I could always feel the soothing comfort of the nearby ocean in the air. Allergies and back-to-back sinus infections had been a huge problem in Sacramento, but now I could breathe deeply again. I discovered a friendly local restaurant and became a regular on the weekend when they had live music. They had a nice outdoor patio, as well as a patient wait staff that didn't mind if I stayed to people-watch long after they cleared the plates. Home at last. I was going to live there forever. For the first time in a long time, I was truly happy.

The only thing missing was a relationship. I wanted to share the next part of my life with someone. I missed the intimacy of being in a long-term relationship. But, as much as I longed for Mr. Wonderful, I'd been putting off doing anything about it until later—after I lost 10 pounds, or learned to speak Italian, or (fill in the blank). Besides, I was much too busy to think seriously about a new relationship. After working my usual 8 hour day, I would put in another 2-3 hours in the evening to make up for wasted time spent in meetings that usually produced little more than a platform for an egotistical president, who loved to pull off his shoes and sit on one foot while pontificating.

My wake-up call came one night after I made the usual dinner run to an Italian restaurant near the office where they knew my name. I couldn't figure out why the restaurant was so crowded, or why there were red balloons hanging from the ceiling. The server reminded me that it was Valentine's Day. Maybe I did need some balance in my life. I signed up for match.com the next day.

Writing the profile had been easy. I'd been through this before with some luck in Sacramento, and still had my recent profile pictures. Match was having a three-months-for-the-price-of-one special, so I immediately signed up before I could change my mind. Then I held my breath.

I didn't have to wait long. Every day I would log in to my account and review responses to my profile. I scrutinized tiny pictures of middle-aged men posing in front of Corvettes, on a boat, or shirtless on the beach. It was obvious that most of them just wanted to get laid by an underwear model, but a few—especially those with young kids—genuinely seemed to want a serious relationship.

I loved kids but I was through with that part of my life, so I skipped over those profiles.

I was getting a fair share of responses, but I didn't want just to be chosen—I wanted to do the choosing as well. After hours of reading hundreds of profiles online, I would find one or two men with potential. One in particular stood out. We had a lot in common, he lived less than 10 miles away, and he had a killer smile. You could tell he had taken time with his profile, so I took a chance on this man who was two years older than I, and still had a teenager at home ("but only for another year or so"). After a few days, he responded back to me by saying, "Thanks, but I'm actually looking for someone 10 years younger."

A word about honesty on the Internet: I was truthful about my age (54 at the time), but many of the men who responded to my profile lied about their age, income bracket, or even their height— all part of the extensive profile questionnaire. I can almost understand fudging a year or two about your age—but lying about your height?

When Paul, who claimed he was 6' tall, met me at the coffee shop, the top of his head barely grazed my chin. I couldn't help myself. After 15 minutes of polite conversation, I had to ask:

"There might be a typo in your profile ..."

"I don't think so. Why do you ask?"

"Your profile said you were 6 feet tall and, well ...." He turned bright red.

"Really? Well, you're not the only one who's disappointed. I was hoping for someone in their 30s."

My jaw hit the table as his ass hit the door.

Then there was Charlie. Charlie was handsome, funny, and in complete denial about still being in love with his ex-wife. I think he was looking for sympathy when he complained about recently snaking out her toilet, while her new boyfriend drank his coffee and read the paper in the next room in his boxers. I should have known when he spent most of our first date talking about his *wife*, not his *ex*-wife.

Next came Roy, whose name I changed to 'Roid when I told the story at work the next day. Roy was not as good looking in person, but seemed intelligent and kept up his side of the conversation—until he got drunk at dinner, pointed to my chest and asked, "Are those things real?"

I was optimistic about an art gallery owner from Beverly Hills, who insisted that we meet in spite of the distance between us—45 minutes on a good day and up to 90 minutes in L.A. traffic. I wanted a local man without the hassle of a commute that would interfere with spontaneity (did he not read my profile preferences?), but he was relentless. I reluctantly agreed to dinner and we got along great for the next three weeks. I let my guard down long enough to invite him to a company event. Two days before the party, he called to say it was not working because we just lived too far apart.

The last straw came after corresponding for several weeks with a nice guy who lived only 10 miles away. When we finally decided to meet in person, he stood me up not once, but twice, calling afterwards to beg forgiveness and ask for a third chance. I politely told him I was no longer interested. After a moment of silence, he called me a bitch and hung up. After two months of disillusionment and disappointment, I pulled the plug. A girl can only drink so much coffee with strangers.

Two weeks after I'd canceled my subscription, I was showing the website to a friend who was considering online dating and I was surprised to see that my profile was still active. Not only was it still active, I had a pending inquiry in my Inbox!

Good ol' Traveling Man Frank. Apparently, I'd checked the box to "cancel upon expiration" rather than scrolling to the bottom of the page to "cancel immediately." His short note ended with, "If you'd rather not respond, I understand, and still wish you the best of luck in finding someone special." His picture showed a handsome man posing in front of a restaurant in New York (fully clothed, with neither a boat nor Corvette in sight). There was something about his eyes; they had a sparkle that hinted at a good sense of humor and tenderness. What the hell. I jumped in again.

"Wouldn't you know it? A handsome man finally responds after I thought I'd canceled my subscription," I wrote. "Here's my personal email address if you still want to talk—but hurry. The subscription expires for real at the end of the week."

The rest, as they say, is history.

He described himself as a public servant, loved music from the '50s, and was a huge New York Yankees fan. He poked fun at himself and believed "The best was yet to be." He didn't consider himself an extravagant person, but always got the best seats in the house for concerts or baseball games ("Nothing but the best for me and my match"). Unfortunately, he lived in a desert community exactly 83 miles from my front door, yet had somehow snuck through the geographic filter. He later promised to do the lion's share of the commuting, if things went well. His three kids were grown and gone, as was my daughter. One son, with whom he was close and visited regularly, lived 10 miles from me in Oxnard. He sounded sincere, adventurous, and somewhat romantic. If my friend from work had not asked about my experience with online dating, I would never have seen the response from Traveling Man Frank. Maybe the universe was trying to throw me a bone.

We had a couple of phone conversations and emailed each other every day for three weeks before deciding to meet in person. I told him I was nervous about testing our chemistry because I'd really enjoyed things so far. He admitted the same thought had crossed his mind, but we had to meet at some point—how about dinner next Saturday, somewhere casual with a great view of the water?

Wanting to keep a low profile, I only told two people at work about "Mr. Wonderful." On Saturday afternoon, I cleaned the house, went grocery shopping, and changed clothes 5 times. At the last minute, I ditched my shoes for cowboy boots. It was the first time I'd given a blind date my home address instead of meeting in a public place, and I started to get cold feet as the day wore on. Both dogs charged the front door at the sound of the doorbell. I took a deep breath and hesitated for just a moment before opening the door.

"Well, girls," I said to Molly and Emily, my Golden Retrievers. "This could be really good or really bad."

CHAPTER 3

PRE-TRIP POWER STRUGGLES

We were getting closer and closer to the start of our road trip. The latest arguments were over how to pack things for long-term storage. We had two very different approaches when it came to our 10' x 30' storage unit (which would also have to store my Honda CRV); he was more focused on using the space effectively, while I insisted on a strategic plan to protect the few things I had left.

"You have to wrap the oak hutch in a blanket or it will warp! The car has to be on jacks, or the tires will bulge after a year in one spot! You have to cover the red leather chair in a blanket—and no boxes stacked on the seat! The mattresses have to be put into plastic sleeves and sealed in special boxes or the mice will get them!"

He was just as exasperated with me.

"Calm down," he said. "I know what I'm doing."

He was stacking boxes 5-high and jamming lamps wherever he could find space. He thought it was ridiculous to go to so much trouble for the mattresses, so he slid them upright and naked between the washing machine and the dryer. It felt like he fought me every step of the way whenever I tried to take the lead on how to organize and prepare our things for storage. We both thought the other was micro managing. More than once, I would find myself behind a locked bathroom door, crying into a towel.

I can't help it; I get attached to people, places, and things. I loved my friends from work; the lemon tree I received as a housewarming gift after moving to Thousand Oaks; the blue handkerchief with embroidered angels that my mom gave me when I was a little kid; and places surrounded by green hills, with a hint of ocean in the air. Houses have always been a huge attachment. Their spirits linger long after the moving truck pulls away.

I was at a crossroads. I had been slowly dismantling my old life right down to the foundation. As each garbage bin filled, I felt a sense of relief at getting rid of clutter, but also trepidation. I'd been ruthless—ripping the Band-Aid off, rather than peeling it down slowly. I constantly wondered what I'd accidentally thrown out that I should have kept.

While throwing out *the old*, I was simultaneously living on faith that *the new* would be better. However, *the new* was at least a year away and we had no idea where we would live after the trip. In the meantime, I was walking away from things I loved and had spent decades acquiring for my home. I agreed to move from my house in Thousand Oaks to his house in the desert, and subsequently became overwhelmed by isolation, depression, and loneliness. The strain of traveling for work, dealing with work and home drama, and constantly feeling like my clothes were itchy and two sizes too small, took a heavy toll.

Of course, arguing about how to prepare items for storage was just a smoke screen. We were about to leave our careers, families, and friends, to spend 12 months together while traveling across

America in a small RV with our dog. He had no fear of the unknown and embraced it.

I questioned what I was giving up, and why.

CHAPTER 4
THE STORY OF US - THE EARLY DAYS

After weeks of flirting through email, I answered the door and we saw each other in person for the first time. We were both instantly smitten.

I would learn that Frank was his Karaoke name and his real name was Howard. He kept a low profile because he worked for the court system and wanted to maintain his privacy. When I opened the door, I felt an immediate rush of relief and attraction (so much for worrying about chemistry). He was 6'1" tall and looked a little like a runner—not overly buff, but very fit and at ease in his body. His hair was still more pepper than salt, and he had one of those groomed 5 o'clock shadows—a little scruffy, but sexy. We hugged hello very naturally and exchanged compliments. He didn't seem to mind the dogs circling like goldfish around his legs and bent down to scratch their heads.

I immediately liked him.

We had a quick glass of wine before heading to Long Beach for dinner. It was at least a two-hour drive, so I was curious as to why he had chosen Long Beach. He said he had been to this restaurant with a group from work and liked it so much that he wanted to come back someday to share it with someone special. I beamed.

During the long drive, we had a chance to get to know each other. We shared our early history and agreed that we had both passed the statute of limitations on divorce horror stories, so we skipped those. He was a year older than I was and had three grown children to my one grown daughter. I learned that his two sons, Matt and Mike, were in California, and his daughter, Danielle, lived in Austin, Texas. Matt was married and had a teenage stepdaughter, as well as a 2-year old daughter with his wife, Maria. They lived in Oxnard, just 10 miles from my front door. I told him about my 24-year-old daughter, Lyndsay, who'd moved to Hollywood after graduating from Long Beach State a year earlier.

Howard said he had been divorced for a very long time and had recently ended a long-term relationship. He would never have signed up for match.com on his own, but his son convinced him to try it. I was the second woman he called. The first broke down in tears over the phone because she missed her ex-husband.

"I must have looked pretty good after that!" I teased.

"You looked pretty good from the first time I saw your picture and read your profile," he said with a smile.

He was handsome *and* charming, too? This had a prayer.

Once we got to the restaurant, he led the way through a crowded parking lot, and took my hand as we navigated our way through the sea of cars. I noticed my heart did a little flutter when he touched me. "Down, girl," I thought to myself.

It was a typical evening in Southern California. We watched the sun set over the ocean from an outdoor table on the deck of the restaurant. The dinner conversation flowed without effort, but we were also comfortable in silence. It felt as though we had known each other for a long time.

We held hands again on the drive home as we listened to music. When we got back to my place, I invited him in for a tour of my townhouse. While we were standing on the balcony, looking at the lights of the city below, he kissed me. It was a soft, sweet kiss. We looked into each other's eyes for a long moment, before he suddenly said he had to go.

Wow.

As soon as he got back to his house, he emailed me to say that he'd had a great time and ask if I was busy the following Saturday. On our second date, we picked right up from where we left off the week before. He was funny, smart, and very attentive. This time, dinner consisted of a Dodger Dog and a beer at a baseball game. I can't remember if the Dodgers won or lost that night, but I do remember that we had a lot of fun and that it felt very natural to be together. The following Saturday he came to my house with an overnight duffle bag. We spent every weekend together, from Friday night to Monday morning, for the next 12 months. We were stupid-in-love, talked for hours, and touched constantly. After a year, he officially moved in with me in Thousand Oaks.

Howard commuted from my place to his work—164 miles round trip—every day for the next 18 months. The stress of the commute added to an already rough adjustment period, after both having lived alone for many years. Neither of us was prepared for the difficulty of merging our lives together. I was used to entertaining friends, while he was exhausted and craved privacy after work. I missed the romance of our long courtship. He missed being able to come home during lunch for a nap. The commute was really beginning to wear him down; he fell asleep at the wheel twice and woke up just in time to avoid an accident. There were also serious problems at my work. I wanted him to comfort me, rather than tell me what to do to fix the situation—typical man/woman stuff. We had lived alone for so long that we had trouble adjusting to boundaries and having to compromise. I was seriously beginning to doubt the wisdom of our moving in together.

Pressure continued to build. I changed companies and my new position required a lot of travel. When I wasn't in my home office, I was on an airplane. He resented the commute and couldn't understand why I was unwilling to rent my place out so we could move into his place. It made sense on paper, but I refused to budge. I loved Thousand Oaks and, frankly, wasn't crazy about the desert where he had a condominium.

It was 2009. His retirement was just a year away and he promised me that we could live anywhere I wanted after that. To sweeten the pot, he suggested that I bank my paychecks for that year as insurance. If things didn't work out, he reasoned, I would have a nest egg with which to start again. Having lost my 401k during the tech-stock era, this offer was hard to turn down. I didn't want to go, but I knew he'd made up his mind about moving back. It was either go with him, or go back to square one with the duffle bag every weekend.

After arguing for months, I finally gave in. Once the decision was made, things moved very quickly. My new property manager immediately found tenants for my townhouse. Next, I sold the furniture that was too big for his place. Everything was moving much too fast, but I tried not to dwell on it. We had a lot of good things going for us. I had to give this relationship a chance, or live with the consequences (whatever those were). My head said it was a good decision, but it broke my heart to leave the one place in which I had felt completely at home. My spirit screamed that I was making a huge mistake, so I turned my back on it.

CHAPTER 5

LIVING IN THE DESERT

I t was even worse than I imagined. Although his condominium was a nice 3-bedroom, two-story townhouse (with a landscaped back yard full of native plants), the drive through town to get there was depressing. We lost one of the dogs, Molly, to cancer the year before, so now there was just Emily. There was no grass for her, so Howard had pea gravel (no pun intended) poured in the narrow side yard. He didn't like the idea of a dog door, and said we would leave the back slider open for her to come in and out as she pleased. I wondered what we would do during the summer when temperatures routinely reached over 100 degrees for days on end. Surely, we would have to keep the door closed because of the air conditioner—something else I hated. When I left Sacramento, I swore I would never breathe refrigerated air again, which was no problem in Thousand Oaks, but a big problem in the desert.

Howard was sympathetic at first. He surprised me by having the kitchen and living room painted in the same colors as my place in Thousand Oaks. He tried to do other things that would make me happy, but I was still miserable. Sometimes I had to leave at 4 am to catch an early flight out of Burbank. However, there was a silver lining because, for once, I didn't mind getting out of town for business travel.

I was dumbfounded as to how I ended up living in the exact opposite of where I'd planned to spend the rest of my life. I left Sacramento to get away from dry heat and to be closer to the ocean. Thousand Oaks had nourished my dry sinuses, as well as my soul. I knew better—how had I allowed this to happen?

In fairness, the town had changed a lot from the early days. My husband spent many years enjoying the beauty of sunsets that stretched uninterrupted for miles over the desert landscape. Old timers were quick to reminisce about how peaceful it used to be there. In the beginning, I really did try to see the good when possible. The city had successfully redesigned the downtown area to include Friday night concerts, a pedestrian mall, and a weekly Farmers Market. However, nothing could compensate for the sheer misery I felt upon waking most mornings, to realize where I was. I could never get used to the expansiveness of the landscape; Howard admired the wide-open vistas and relative lack of traffic. I saw only tumbleweeds and dust storms, and bit my tongue. There was a constant wind from the west, especially at dusk when my allergies would peak. It wasn't safe to ride my bike five blocks to the grocery store, or walk the dog alone after dark, because of gang activity.

Someone at a party once tried to explain how the demographics had changed after the new prison opened. Suddenly, many nomadic people moved into the area to be closer to their incarcerated family members. There was also a spike in the number of homeless people around this time, some in need of treatment for mental illness or addiction, and others existing on whatever change could be had from panhandling. Speaking of which, it was impossible for me to walk from the parking lot to the grocery store without being stalked for spare change. They must have sensed that I was an easy mark (they were right) since I usually kept money in my pocket for those times.

The conversation would go something like this, without taking a breath:

"I need $4.37 to get enough gas to get to my brother's house because his wife is in the hospital and I promised I'd babysit his kids while he visited her but I ran out of gas and barely made it to the parking lot and if you give me your address I'll pay you back as soon as I get paid next week."

Sometimes I would be short on cash and hand them a buck, which would prolong the conversation.

"Gee, a whole dollar. Really? This won't get me to my sister's house."

"I thought you said it was your brother's house?"

"No. No. You heard it wrong."

And so it went …

I should have known what I was getting into, because we would occasionally spend time at his place before Howard moved in with me. Of course, I'd noticed negative things back then, but noticing them and actually living there, were completely different.

After I got unpacked during the first week in my new home, Howard asked me if I wanted to go out for a drink and get to know the town. He was trying to cheer me up, so I put on lipstick, changed my clothes, and looked forward to a few hours in a nice bar or restaurant. I was a little startled when he turned onto a side street leading out of town and into the open desert. He smiled when I made a joke about looking for a place to dig a shallow grave. We drove for about a half an hour with nothing but the moon for illumination until we reached a small bar in the middle of the desert **with an airplane impaled through the roof!** Welcome to the iconic Wing and a Prayer Bar.

After Howard turned off the car in the parking lot, I just stared at him. The moment we walked into the brightly lit bar, 30 strangers stopped talking and turned towards us in unison. Action at the pool table froze, as I calculated how many steps it would take to make it back to the car. After giving the stink-eye to us for a min-ute, people got back to their business. We found two open seats at the bar and I immediately tried to catch the bartender's eye—I needed a drink. He was doing a good job of ignoring me, but that didn't stop Howard from making friends with a bearded man to his right. Meanwhile, I was having a stare-down with a biker chick who was chalking-up her cue stick. I figured I'd better get my bad-ass attitude on so she wouldn't think I was dainty. Meanwhile, Mr. Wonderful was making friends with the bartender. Eventually, I passed time by sipping an ice-cold glass of shitty wine, as clear as a glass of water, while glaring back at anyone who looked my way.

This would become our pattern over the next two years: Howard was the good guy, and I was the one who didn't belong.

In all honesty, it was my problem, not theirs. I am sure 90% of the folks in the bar that night were good people (glaring-pool-cue-biker-chick might have been the exception). I was an asshole with an attitude, and didn't even try to hide it.

In my own defense—a remote bar in the middle of the desert? He should have given me a heads-up; I would have left the good jewelry at home and had a couple of Tequila shots before leaving the house.

Later that same week, I noticed a deeply tanned older woman wearing raggedy shorts and a faded tank top. She was also wearing huge headphones and dancing on the sidewalk. She was pump-ing her arms, swinging her legs, and really working up a sweat. Actually, you wouldn't really call it dancing—perhaps it was some kind of music workout? Was she waiting for the cross walk light to change? Nope. Howard told me that she was one of several local characters who may, or may not, have mental issues. She was on the same street corner every day, dancing to her heart's content. He didn't think the headphones were plugged into anything, and speculated that maybe the mother ship provided her background music.

There was also a different dress code going on there. I was used to seeing the occasional teenager at the mall in Thousand Oaks wearing stylish flannel pajama pants, sparkly flip-flops, and a clean, matching tank top. I was not used to seeing a grown woman in a full set of old flannel pajamas—complete with nasty, matted, faux-fur bedroom slippers— waiting in line with us at the movies.

"Howard," I hissed. "Look! Look!"

"What?"

"That lady in line behind us is wearing pajamas and slippers!"

"Uh-huh. I guess she wants to be comfortable."

He was used to it; I was horrified daily.

However, it was not just the colorful people; it was also the dangerous people. A man was stabbed in the neck with a meat thermometer at the local movie theater because he asked a woman to stop using her cell phone during the movie, and it offended the woman's boyfriend. Why a meat thermometer, you ask? According to the newspaper, he was on parole and not allowed to carry a gun or a knife.

As time went on, I noticed that some of the locals seemed to get a kick out of my discomfort. I stuck out as being from "Down Below," which referred to anything in or around Los Angeles. To make things worse, I didn't sugarcoat how much I hated it there (which I regret today). However, I wasn't the only one. I met only one person who had memories of the good old days and said he still liked it there just fine. In a quieter voice, he also said he had nowhere else to go. Although people approached me at parties with whispers of "I hate this fucking place, too," the difference was that they had earned the right to their opinion. I was a newcomer and I should have been more polite.

Whether I was at a party, the grocery store, or walking my dog, someone would inevitably ask, "So, how do you like living here?"

I would start out diplomatically. "It's been an adjustment."

Once, one of Howard's poker buddies teased me and said, "I hear you miss Nordstrom."

"And they miss me," I answered, still trying to be polite.

"You'll get used to it in about 10 years!"

Depending on how much I'd had to drink, I would usually let it slide, or counter with a snarky remark about slitting my wrists first.

After a while, I just told the truth. It was one of the few times in my life when I didn't care what people thought of me.

I had to keep reminding myself that it was only fair; I worked out of the house. Howard only had a year left before retirement (or so we thought). Why should he continue commuting from my place, when his house was five minutes from his office? We both knew I could live anywhere, as long as there was an airport nearby.

One year turned into two when Howard's retirement plan changed, and staying an extra year would yield a more favorable pension. Even though I knew better, I felt as though I'd been tricked. I was not only miserable at the thought of another year in the desert, but also deeply depressed about it. Howard's way of dealing with conflict was to "walk it off," as though a brisk walk around the neighborhood held all the answers (sometimes it does). If that didn't work, he would try ignoring me when I was in what he called "one of my moods." Finally, he would try distraction, which just further irritated me. Rather than talk things out, his default reaction to conflict was to suggest that we "just try to have a good day." It's a man thing.

I lost a lot of sleep during those two+ years while feeling sorry for myself, mulling over arguments, and obsessing over the shitty parts of my life, on an endless loop. I'd been battling insomnia for years, but this brought on a completely new dimension of sleep-deprivation. I cannot count the number of times I was up all night after an argument, revising my part of the fight to say what I *really* meant, and wondering if I'd made a huge mistake.

Meanwhile, Mr. Wonderful snored away next to me—another man/woman thing, according to my girlfriends, who had experienced the same thing.

I was also very lonely. I made a friend who hated the place almost as much as I did, but our schedules didn't line up very often. Even when the two of us could get away without the husbands, she had to run home in time to make her husband's dinner, or soothe him after a rough day. She was not only struggling with living in the desert, but also commuting over a hundred miles a day for her job in L.A., and grappling with newlywed adjustments. I was hoping for wine and laughter; she needed a shoulder and a friend.

I was isolated and lonely, but Howard had friends everywhere! I teased him about never being able to have an affair because we ran into people he knew every time we went out in public. It was still a small town, in spite of a population of well over 100,000 people. In addition to work friends, he had a poker group, which had been meeting once a month for over a decade. His roots went deep and I was happy for him. I felt so guilty for not adapting. Although his work friends were very gracious to me, it would have been awkward to be friends outside the office with the boss's girlfriend.

I was sleep-deprived, physically exhausted, burned out from too much travel for work, unsure of the future of this relationship, lonely, and hated where we lived—not what you would call in a good place. It wasn't much fun for Howard, either.

But it wasn't all bad, because we got out of town almost every weekend. We escaped to Cambria, a little seaside town on the central coast, saw pre-release movies at a great independent movie theater in Pasadena, and spent a lot of time walking on Zuma Beach in Malibu. It was during those times that we inevitably talked about retirement. Howard's dream was to see the country. Forty years in one place was long enough and he, too, counted the days until we could get out.

When he was younger, he wanted to buy a Suburban, throw a mattress in the back, and hit the road for a year or more, stopping at all the major league ballparks. He also wanted to play golf every other day. His early dream did not include anyone else—just the lone wolf and his Suburban. After a round of golf these days, he realized that there was no way his back would survive golf several times a week, so he scratched that off the list. Instead of a Suburban, he bid on a small used RV on Craigslist. One month later, he and his son flew to Chicago and drove it back to California.

Meanwhile, I was still traveling every week for work. The pressure was intense because I was responsible for a field sales team spread over 14 states, with a huge quota, in a depressed market. I was gone at least 3 or 4 days a week, and came home exhausted and resentful. I traveled so much that they knew me at the parking garage of the airport. Coming home from a trip was bittersweet, too. I missed my beautiful townhouse. I missed the fountains and trees of Thousand Oaks, the rolling hills, and the smell of the ocean in the air. I missed normal people, Whole Foods and—yes— Nordstrom. I wanted to stay in the left lane of the highway, back to my *real* home, but instead I had to take the right lane, which would lead to the desert. What had I done? It was no wonder that Howard didn't get off the couch when I walked through the door! He must have dreaded the return of the Unhappy Woman.

Our relationship became fragile at best; something had to change. By this time, my body was beginning to wear out from years of travel and the pressure of corporate life. I had alarming physical symptoms, which resulted in a 3-month medical leave of absence, after which my doctor strongly recommended a complete change of lifestyle—while I still had a choice.

I turned in my retirement papers.

I should have been happy, but it was more complicated than that. I dreamed of spending my retirement years in a little cottage by the sea; the last thing I wanted was more travel. I'd already seen most of the country from 35,000 feet in the air, and through the window of a cab from the airport to the hotel and back again. Maybe traveling for pleasure without deadlines or itineraries wouldn't be so bad after all. Although my company had a regional office in Danbury, Connecticut, I'd never walked in the woods of any state in New England. In fact, New England was one of the few areas I wanted to explore post-retirement, *after* settling in my little place by the sea.

Once we both agreed to retire, the next hurdle was deciding where to live after the road trip. Things got heated when Howard mentioned being open-minded about living in the South. I might not have known exactly where I wanted to live next, but I sure as hell knew where I *didn't* want to live. When I was a kid, my family lived in Alabama during George Wallace's tenure as governor—not the happiest time in my life. No, thank you. Howard reassured me that we had to be in 100% agreement about our next home or we would keep looking. I was concerned that we might even end up moving back to the desert—a definite deal-breaker for our marriage—because he didn't want to sell his condominium in a depressed real estate market. Without a mortgage, I was afraid the temptation of using the desert condo as a home base for future travel would be too strong; he assured me that it was just an investment and promised we would never live there again. In fact, he put California pretty far down the list of options. I couldn't imagine living anywhere outside of California. I especially couldn't imagine living in a different state than my daughter. I didn't want a long distance relationship with my only child. And what about the grandkids—present and future? "That's what airplanes are for," he said, essentially closing the discussion. Seeing the look on my face, he added, "Somehow, it will all work out."

I was not reassured.

Another sore spot was our marital status. When we met, we agreed that marriage was not a priority or even a remote possibility, because we were happy with things the way they were. Between us, we had been through several divorces; we were more than content to live the rest of our lives together without being married. As things progressed, I changed my mind first. We talked about marriage a lot before I moved in with him. We both agreed that we wanted to spend the rest of our lives together. However, if I was going to walk away from my career, sell most of my belongings, and take an extended road trip *without having a house to come home to,* he was going to have to put a little more on the table. To me, an agreement is not quite the same as an engagement. I was just romantic enough to want a proposal.

At first, Howard was ambivalent about marriage because he felt we would always be together whether we were married or not, but it didn't take long before he reconsidered. He told me that the important thing about getting married (besides all of the romantic reasons), was for him to know that I would be taken care of if he died first. I was not aware that the terms of his pension stipulated that we had to be married for a minimum of one year and one day at the time of his retirement for me to be eligible for his death benefits. He was looking out for me. He was taking care of me.

My anxiety, depression, and uncertainty over the future, was tearing us apart. I was tired of thinking, tired of fighting, and very tired of feeling as though my life was in someone else's hands. During a particularly bad bout of insomnia, I set a deadline of June 1 to make a final decision about this relationship—if we weren't all-in by then, I would move back to Thousand Oaks. I loved him dearly and knew he felt the same, but I needed clear communication about our future and he was being evasive.

Little did I know that he was having my wedding ring designed as we were having these long discussions.

CHAPTER 6

MAMA BEAR

I was in a meeting in Los Angeles and glanced down at my silenced phone to see seven missed calls. It was the Friday before the Martin Luther King holiday in 2010, and I was looking forward to a long weekend while also dreading the drive home. Traffic in L.A. on a Friday is a commuter's worst nightmare, even more so before a long weekend. It was common for the freeways to become parking lots during "rush" hour. My usual drive home would normally take a little over two hours this late in the day. However, on that particular Friday, it would be 6 hours before I walked into the house, helping Lyndsay, my badly injured daughter, through the front door.

Most of the missed calls were hang-ups from my daughter and two were from Howard. I kept getting Lyndsay's voice mail; however, Howard answered on the first ring. He calmly told me that she had been in a snowboarding accident at Mountain High Ski Resort, and was on her way to an urgent care center by ambulance. He didn't know the extent of her injuries, just that the ski patrol had to take her off the mountain in a rescue basket. I was in downtown Los Angeles on a Friday afternoon and she was in a mountain town without a hospital more than 80 miles away.

As I squealed out of the parking garage, I hit the first of many gridlocked intersections leading to the freeway. She was my only child and, even though she was a young adult, she still needed me and I couldn't get to her. When I finally reached the freeway, it was also gridlocked. I must have said *fuck* a hundred times during the 3 hours that it took to drive 80 miles.

It was long after dark when I finally pulled into the parking lot of the urgent care center. I barely turned off the car and ran into the lobby, where I saw her sitting in a wheelchair in the waiting area. She was wearing a sling around her right arm and shoulder, while quietly crying with her head down. In that instant, she was my little girl again and I was late picking her up from kindergarten.

It had been an awful fall. The doctor explained that her collarbone was shattered and jagged bone fragments were rubbing against nerves and muscles. The doctors at Urgent Care could not do anything other than put her arm in a sling to minimize movement because she needed surgery, which they were not equipped to perform. They told me to be gentle with her because she screamed throughout the initial exam whenever they moved her. To make matters worse, when I got on the phone with her insurance company to see which hospital she should be taken to and make arrangements for an ambulance, I was told that her HMO required prior approval before she could be admitted to one of their hospitals. According to the woman on the phone, her injuries were not life threatening; the only thing I could do was take her home and wait for preauthorization after the holiday weekend ended on Tuesday. I tried to explain the extent of her pain; she suggested that I take my daughter to the emergency room after we got home—it was probably going to get worse. I hung up, closed my eyes, and took a deep breath. Home was two hours away. The Urgent Care nurse handed us her x-rays and said we could leave the wheelchair in the parking lot.

It was one of the longest weekends of my life. On the ride home, Lyndsay screamed out in pain every time I hit a small bump in the road or carefully turned a corner. Once home, she could barely walk into the house, so I immediately took her to the emergency room. The nurse in the emergency room explained that the hospital had been robbed at gunpoint twice. After the second robbery, they stopped carrying the type of narcotics that would help Lyndsay. They gave her a shot (which did nothing for her pain), suggested Advil as a follow-up, and sent us home.

We both slept sitting up that night—she slept on the couch because it hurt too much to lie down, and I slept on the love seat, next to the couch. We went to a different emergency room the next day with the same result. By the time Tuesday morning finally rolled around, no one had slept more than a few hours at a time. After jumping through a few more hoops—we had to switch her primary care doctor in L.A. for a local doctor who could approve medical treatment—she finally had emergency surgery to repair her collarbone. It took a metal plate and eight screws to piece together the bone; the post-surgery pain was yet another hurdle. During her initial recovery, she lived on our living room couch in constant pain.

Once she was out of danger, Howard became irritable and spent a lot of time away from the house. When he was home, he was incredibly fussy over small things, like what she watched on TV, (he could not stand the "Real Housewives" series). He said he was worried about the demands her recovery placed on me, forgetting that I would take the pain for her if I could. There were many follow-up doctor appointments and countless trips to the drug store to find a painkiller that wouldn't upset her stomach or exasperate her anxiety. I was still working from my home office every day. I tried to balance her needs, his needs, and my work responsibilities. Her dependency and lack of mobility clashed with her ADHD. Howard rationalized that the best way to help me was to stay out of the way. Except he wasn't helping me by staying away—he was making things worse. Yet another item for the laundry list of reasons for me to move back to Thousand Oaks.

The final blow came when one of her roommates called to say that they had 10 days to move because the landlord wanted the house for a family member. I assured them that, legally, the landlord would have to wait until the end of their lease, but it was too late—they had already panicked. Two of the four roommates had moved out, and the third was in the process of packing. We had no choice. On top of everything else, we had to move my daughter out of her place in L.A., move her belongings to storage, deal with shutting off the utilities (all in her name), and fight with the landlord.

I barely spoke to Howard during that awful time. He was hardly ever home, and I didn't have the energy to deal with him when he was. We were at crossroads and it did not look good.

As Lyndsay began to heal, she got very restless. A friend of hers in Hollywood invited her to rent a room in her condominium until she could find a new place; she immediately accepted. Once the pain was under control, I could tell she was bored and felt horrible about "the imposition". No matter how many times I reassured her, she sensed Howard's resentment and wanted to get out of there. Tension continued to escalate. I was furious with Howard for abandoning me when I needed him.

Once we got her settled in her new room in Hollywood, we had a very long and silent drive back to the desert. I must have slept for two days before finally confronting Howard about his behavior. He was shocked at my accusations of abandonment and defended himself by saying he did what he thought was right. He agreed that it was "not the best time" of his life. His defense was that he had no idea how hurt I was over his lack of support.

It turned ugly fast. He accused me of babying my daughter; I accused him of checking out when I needed his help.

I said, "You never <u>once</u> asked if you could go to the drug store for me! Never <u>once</u> did you offer to make dinner! You went to bed without saying good-night <u>and</u> you ate the last banana!"

"You never asked," he countered. "And just listen to the tone of your voice! Who do you think you are? This was no picnic for me either, you know!"

We fought off and on for hours. At one point, I screamed at him that I wanted him to move out. He was dumbfounded and replied, "But, it's *my* place."

"I don't care," I yelled. "Get out!"

It all came together in a perfect storm: the doubts, exhaustion, our terrible communication, and unrealistic expectations on both of our parts.

I fell apart. I was done.

Hours later, we began the long process of fixing our lives, but with very different agendas.

Months earlier, we'd made plans to go to Pebble Beach for the AT&T Pro/Am golf tournament, but after everything we'd been through, I told him I wasn't going. I was sure we were through. I didn't want to spend another hour, let alone a painful weekend, with him. He told me to sleep on it; everything would look different and be okay in the morning. I told him it would never be okay again. After a while, we stopped talking; we had said it all. I went upstairs to lie down and immediately fell asleep. It was dark when I woke up and he was gently rubbing my back.

Where was he weeks earlier when I really needed him? I felt like a truck had hit me. I was so bone-tired that I could barely stand up. I had no energy to argue. I had no energy, period. The last thing I remember mumbling to him before I fell asleep again was, "I'm **not** going to Pebble Beach with you."

However, I was wrong.

In the days following that awful argument, I did nothing but work and sleep. We had a few more conversations about what happened after Lyndsay's accident, and he finally convinced me that regardless of the outcome, we deserved a long weekend at one of the most beautiful beaches in the country. They didn't nick-name Pebble Beach "God's back yard" for nothing.

The truth was that neither one of us was ready to let go. He was wrong not to jump in during the emergency with Lyndsay, but I was also wrong for not telling him what I needed from him. We'd said such horrible things to each other—was it possible to recover? I wasn't sure, but I was sick of over-thinking this relationship. I agreed to go to Pebble Beach with him under one condition: no intense discussions. This would have to be a pure get-away week-end—maybe our last.

Then a funny thing happened a few days before we were sup-posed to leave. First, an interview on TV about incorporating grati-tude into your life caught my eye. Then, I found a book I'd bought years ago based on appreciating what you have instead of focusing on what was lacking in your life. Finally, my Kindle highlighted a book called *Marry Him*, by Lori Gottlieb, who "… set out to see if the problem is not a dearth of good men, but rather women's ex-pectations of them."

Was the universe trying to tell me something? I downloaded the book on my Kindle and read it in the car on the way to Pebble Beach. As I read, something inside of me slowly began to soften.

CHAPTER 7
PEBBLE BEACH ENGAGEMENT

Howard proposed to me on the beach in Carmel. We woke up early on Valentine's Day and decided to take a quick walk on the beach before showering and getting ready for the rest of the day. I pulled my ponytail through the back of my baseball hat, laced up my walking shoes, and skipped the lipstick altogether. It didn't take long to walk from our hotel to the beach through movie-set beautiful neighborhoods. Gone was all trace of tension. After the drama of the past few months, we were finally back to being us again. He picked up a stick and began writing in the sand, but it wasn't until I noticed an expectant look on his face that I read what he had written:

"I love you and want to marry you."

My heart stopped.

Just to be sure, I said, "Would you please phrase that in the form of a question?"

He laughed, kissed me, and opened a black velvet box that held a white-gold wedding band embedded with 12 diamonds—"one for each month of the year that I will love you." Not only had he chosen each of the diamonds himself; he had also designed the way they fit flush into the band.

I said yes.

On March 20, only 5 weeks later, we were married in a small ceremony at a resort on a cliff overlooking the water, as the fog rolled in over the ocean. Being married put the road trip into perspective and added the sense of security that I needed to make the changes that were coming.

Life was good.

CHAPTER 8

THE JOURNEY BEGINS

I felt a great sense of relief, as I looked at the passenger-side mirror from the front seat of the RV with Emmy asleep on the couch behind Howard. The desert town that had been my reluctant home for over two years was slowly dissolving into the surrounding landscape; no tears were shed.

Our first stop was Newbury Park, near my old Thousand Oaks stomping grounds. We were going to spend the night with our friends, Lee and Gigi, who had been our witnesses when we got married. Gigi and I had met several years earlier at the office in Thousand Oaks and developed a friendship. I even had a small part in Lee's surprise marriage proposal; so when it came time to think about our witnesses, we thought of them.

The plan was to spend one night with Lee and Gigi, before driving another hour up the coast to Oxnard to spend a night with Howard's son, Matt, and his family. Afterwards, we would be stopping in Lompoc for a few days to visit my brother, Tom, and his wife, Lina. Then it was off to Nipomo to visit Larry and Bonney, friends from Howard's work, who had retired a few years ahead of us. Our first stop that did not involve family or friends would be

San Simeon—home of Hearst Castle near Cambria, one of our favorite romantic weekend get-away destinations.

The visit with Lee and Gigi was fun in spite of feeling as though we were intruding on them. It was just a week after the birth of their new son, but Gigi insisted that we come for the night. One look at the new parents reminded me of how overwhelming those early days (and nights) could be. We tried to be good guests by having dinner delivered and said goodnight shortly after dessert.

Although we had taken several short trips in the RV, this would be our first official night of sleeping in Sonward (named after us: Son for SONja and Ward for HoWARD); but instead of an RV Park, we were going to plug an extension cord from their garage to Sonward and park in the street in front of their house. The extension cord allowed us to have electricity for the lights, and because we were only spending one night, we did not hook-up water for the toilet or sinks. Feeling pretty smug ("This is gonna be easy!"), we giggled and kept checking the curtains for cracks as we undressed, converted the couches into a king-size bed with the push of a button, and talked about how this would soon become our bedtime ritual.

The next morning we both woke up with full bladders. We gently knocked on the door, but everyone was still asleep. After putting our bedding away, I slapped on some deodorant and pulled on yesterday's clothes. My teeth were a little grimy and I could taste last night's wine on my tongue, but I'd gone a day without showering before and it hadn't killed me. I could do this.

After a desperate run to the restroom, I saved an outside table at Starbucks as Howard got his oatmeal and my coffee. As I was waiting, it slowly began to dawn on me that we were *really* doing it—we were taking off on what most people would consider to be the trip of a lifetime. It felt liberating! The whole world was waiting (well, at least the U.S.). Why had I been so anxious? This was going to be great! We would see inspirational scenery for the blog, and finally have time for long talks and leisurely sex. We would listen to music and talk about all the things that we had been too distracted in our old lives to resolve. Not everyone could spend so much time together, but we were different. We were going to rock it, in spite of what friends jokingly referred to as the Ultimate Marriage Test.

We finished our breakfast and went back to the house to leave a good-bye note on the door. New parents needed all the sleep they could get.

Later that day, everyone was in high spirits during our visit with son, Matt, his wife, Maria, and granddaughters, Nicole and Madison. I was happy to sleep in Madison's bed instead of Sonward and took a long shower the next morning after everyone left for work. After breakfast, it was a short drive for a long walk on the beach at the Mandalay Bay Resort before we ventured further up the coast. We stopped for lunch in Santa Barbara and later took a winding country road through the hills outside of Lompoc to watch the wind surfers at Jalama Beach.

It was not until we hit Lompoc to visit my brother that it dawned on me: I no longer had my own shower. Bathing whenever I wanted was over—ditto for doing laundry. We would have to stop at coin-operated Laundromats every week or so, which meant that I would have to get used to wearing the same clothes several days in a row. No problem—fewer options meant fewer decisions, which translated into simplicity, one of the benefits of our road trip. Besides, it is not as though I had to dress for work anymore. I could wear a pair of jeans for a week, as long as I was careful not to spill anything on them. As for tops, I'd packed several short and long-sleeved t-shirts to wear on the road, as well as a few sweatshirts. I would take a European bath if I had to (freshening-up with a washcloth).

In reality, Sonward was designed for use on short-trips—it was not built for cross-country exploration. After running out of hot water in the middle of shampooing my hair, it didn't take long to learn that it was easier to wait for a full-service RV Park to shower—ditto for using the toilet for anything other than peeing emergencies.

In order to use our tiny and cumbersome toilet, we had to step on one pedal to slightly fill the bowl with water from an onboard storage tank, do the deed, then step on a different pedal to flush, which would store the "black" water in a separate tank until we could get to a dump station. I was going to have to get over my squeamishness about using public restrooms, as well as learn to embrace public showers. I made a mental note to buy a pair of shower flip-flops on our next shopping trip.

My brother's house in Lompoc was a welcoming sanctuary. It was only day four of our trip, but I could already feel the transition from stressed-out to blissed-out. I was finally living in the moment, rather than ruminating about the past, or worrying about the future. Emily was a little confused about the new routine, but literally jumped for joy at seeing Bella, their Chocolate Lab. Lina is an amazing cook and kept our bellies full during our three-day visit. We drank wine, stayed up late, compared childhood memories, and laughed a lot. The guys argued good-naturedly about who had been the best guitarist in the 1970s, while Lina and I were catching up on our kids' lives. During the day, while Tom and Lina were at work, Howard and I walked the dogs or made a grocery run. We felt at home there. Eighteen months later, it would actually become our home for three weeks.

On the last day of our visit, the four of us took a hike in the Santa Ynez Mountains to scatter a small portion of my dad's cremains in an area he found particularly interesting. My father was a German rocket scientist, lifelong nature-lover, and insatiable traveler. His cremains were supposed to launch into space, but those plans fell through after years of delays by the private space company. After he retired from aerospace, my dad had his own company and developed instruments with great accuracy that could detect minerals, oil, and water, either from the ground or from the sky in an airplane. He constantly recalibrated and adjusted them in the field, right up until his death in 2002 at age 96. There was one particular spot in the Santa Ynez Mountains that made his instruments "go funny" (his words) in a Bermuda-Triangle sort of way. We hiked to that very spot, thanks to my brother's sharp memory, and released a small amount of his cremains to the wind while Elton John's *Rocket Man* played in my mind.

I will never forget the silence of the valley below, and the way the wind swirled tiny specks of what looked like course sand into the sky before they disappeared. We would continue this ritual throughout the country, scattering his cremains during visits to national parks, peaceful lakes, into the sea, and other places he would have loved.

We left Lompoc with lots of good memories and headed straight up the coast, past San Simeon, to Pinnacles National Monument (now a national park) near King City. We were being true to our mission of not necessarily taking the fastest routes, as we drove 30 miles from King City to Pinnacles on a beautiful back road also known as Highway 25. We saw hundreds of black, white, and brown cows, happily grazing on the side of steep cliffs. I'd always taken Highway 101 to visit my parents in Lompoc; I didn't know this road existed.

Pinnacles Monument is an ancient volcanic field made up of massive monoliths, spires, and sheer-walled canyons, due to millions of years of erosion, faulting and tectonic plate movement. It was both beautiful and haunting. We had no trouble finding the Visitor Center to pick up a trail map. We took Emmy for a quick walk before getting her settled in the air conditioned RV for a nap while we hiked in the heat. After a quick lunch under a shady canopy of trees, we packed about four ounces of my dad's cremains in a baggie and hiked 1.7 miles to Condor Gulch Lookout.

While we were hiking, I began thinking about the stormy relationship I'd had with my father. People who knew us both said we were alike in many ways—stubborn, argumentative, unwilling or incapable of censoring our words when passions ran high. On the other hand, the same people said we were also highly intelligent, creative, had a good sense of humor, and needed change on a regular basis. Maybe that's why we clashed so often during my teen years; before then, I was afraid of him and left the room whenever he entered it. He was much older than my friends' fathers (almost 50 when I was born) and spoke in extremely broken English, when he spoke at all. He was of the generation that believed "children should be seen and not heard" and would smack first, rarely asking questions later. My dad and I had our first conversation of substance after my mother died in 1999, because she was no longer there to run interference for him. In spite of the difficulty we had in communicating, I was fiercely loyal to him and loved him dearly.

As we began our ascent, I told Howard about a greeting card that my father had uncharacteristically given me when I was a teenager. My mother was the nurturer of the family and took care of everything, especially special occasions that required a greeting card, so this was a first. The card said, "Even when I'm mad at you, I love you." He wrote a brief German quote. As Howard and I silently struggled up a rocky path, I remembered asking my mother what it said. She told me it was part of a poem by Goethe, called "*The Elf King*" (also known as "*Der Erlkönig*"). After my father died, I looked it up online and realized what he was trying to tell me. The poem was about a father who rode through the night with a sick child. Death whispers to the child throughout the trip, disguised as fog, wind rustling through dry leaves, and an old willow tree. The father shudders when his child tells him he sees the Elf King (death) and rides harder, but it is too late—the child dies in his father's arms.

My father had little use for affection or words of encourage-
ment, so this poem was especially meaningful to me, because it
was his way of saying that he loved me.

We finally made it to Condor Gulch Lookout with a beautiful valley below. Even though eight years had passed since my
father's death, I cried silent tears as I released his cremains to
the wind, watching them blow into rocks, over trees, and into a
pool of water below. Later that day, I noticed a small silver grain
of sand stuck to my t-shirt, near my heart.

We were hot, sweaty, and slightly dehydrated, by the time
we hiked all the way back to Sonward. Maybe that's why we decided to push on to Santa Cruz instead of spending the night
at Pinnacles—big mistake.

After hours of winding roads in the Santa Cruz Mountains, we
finally found the RV Park we were looking for. It was highly rated
in our *Trailer Life Directory of RV Parks and Campgrounds,* and had
full hook-ups (water, sewer and electric) as well as a small coffee
shop in their general store. It might have been nice during the
day, but it was almost midnight when we got there, and we were
tired, hungry, and grumpy, after a long day. Because it was too
dark to see, we had to park Sonward and set out on foot to try to
find the office. We finally stumbled onto it and, of course, it was
closed. Using our cell phones as flashlights, we looked for the af-
ter-hours instructions, usually posted on the door, but there were
none. After more than a few expletives, we gave up and headed
back to Sonward. It took another hour of driving around Santa
Cruz before we finally gave up searching for a dog-friendly hotel
for the night. That night was the first time we snuck Emmy into a
hotel room. She left less of a footprint than most humans did, but
policy is policy.

You may be wondering why we didn't just pull over by the side
of the road for the night, or find a Walmart parking lot. We talked
about it, but I was nervous about parking on the side of a narrow

mountain road. As for Walmart, my research indicated that not all Walmarts were RV friendly, and I didn't want to take a chance on having to answer a knock on the door by a 20-year-old security guard in the middle of the night. We skipped dinner and called it a night.

Next stop: Sacramento!

CHAPTER 9

HOMETOWN BLUES

As we were approaching Sacramento on our way to South Lake Tahoe to visit my daughter, Lyndsay, and her boyfriend, Jeff, I realized that this was only the second time Howard and I had been to Sacramento together. The first time was on the way to Lee and Gigi's wedding the year before, when we made a very quick stop there for lunch, but didn't do any sight-seeing. This time we had several hours to kill, so we decided to visit Old Sacramento, the town of Folsom, and Folsom Lake, before heading to Tahoe—just in time for Lyndsay and Jeff to get off work. I was thrilled that Howard was going to see my old haunts.

We got into a silly argument that I can't even remember now, and I saw Sacramento perhaps the way he had seen the city in the desert where we lived for over two years. When he complained about the traffic, I got defensive. He insisted that Sacramento was humid; I argued it was dry. We were both just blowing off steam because of too much togetherness. Had we been at home, I would have taken off to Target for a few hours (because there's always something you need at Target) and he probably would have gone to the local poker room with his son, Mike. However, we had nowhere to go, so we sniped at each other. It was good for me to see my hometown through his eyes and realize just how much criticism he had put up with from me during the previous two+ years.

We walked stiffly through Old Sacramento. I passed the restaurant with the brick patio where I once sat alone on one of the weekends Lyndsay spent with her dad, listening to live jazz, and hoping that someone like Howard would come into my life. I told Howard about the first time I took my daughter to the Old Railroad Museum, and Frank Fat's Restaurant, where I held my mom's hand as we navigated the stairs in search of a bathroom. Next was the Firehouse Restaurant, where they knew my order by heart when I was pregnant, and began slicing strawberries the moment I walked through the door. I told him about turning my ankle on the cobblestone streets one New Year's Eve back in the 1980s. I went on and on, as the memories came flooding back. Howard was quiet.

Once we got to the town of Folsom, I was hit with another unexpected wave of nostalgia. My girlfriends and I spent hours on the second story patio of a Mexican restaurant, drinking pitchers of Margarita's, and laughing our asses off. I remembered a first date with a great guy at the white-linen-tablecloth restaurant just around the corner. I also thought about the schools I'd visited in Folsom when I was a field sales rep, before going into management, and the relief I'd felt upon finally finding a job that was not only a good fit, but also provided a career track and excellent compensation package.

I'd lived in the Sacramento area for over 35 years before moving to Thousand Oaks, and I was surprised by the tender feelings I had for my old hometown. On previous visits, a cloud of depression wrapped itself around me from painful memories having to do with being a single mother there. I felt like a failure in Sacramento—Thousand Oaks had given me a new start.

Howard wanted to take a short hike along the American River; I wanted to be in nice clothes waiting for a table on the patio. He needed to stretch his legs, while I felt like an unmade bed, tangled up in memories. We took a short hike, shot a few photographs, and headed to Folsom Lake after splitting a deli sandwich for lunch.

The lake was nothing like I remembered. When I first moved to Sacramento in the 1970s, Folsom Lake was a vacation destination. You had to hustle to get a reservation at the campground and there were very long lines at the boat launch. A friend from work had a sailboat and taught me how to navigate by reading the wind on my back. Years later, I met a man with a boat who took me on dinner dates to the middle of the lake. He would drop anchor and play classical music while we shared a bottle of wine before the sun went down.

Now Folsom Lake looked like a small, sad puddle in the middle of a dry riverbed. Gone were the dark waves with white caps that I remembered. Howard wanted to take Emily for a walk before we headed to South Lake Tahoe, but I'd had enough for one day and stayed behind. I waited 15 minutes after they left before trying to find them in my binoculars. There they were—two tiny specks held together by a red leash. Even from that distance, I could tell he was happy: a boy and his dog. Fighting some unnamed sadness, I slipped back into Sonward, intending to read my Kindle until they got back, and instead found myself opening the freezer where I kept the vodka.

CHAPTER 10

MY DAUGHTER'S FATHER

It didn't take long before my trip down memory lane took a hard turn for the worse. I thought being in Sacramento with my husband would give him the opportunity to understand me on a deeper level, as if tracing my footsteps would spark an interest in all the things we mutually agreed not to discuss—like prior relationships and dramatic stories of what went wrong in our previous marriages. My demons were alive and kicking as we accidentally drove by a former house I shared with my daughter's father. The emotional whiplash that followed was instantaneous and intense.

It was raining that day in 1984, when I joined my future-ex-husband and father of our 3-year-old daughter for lunch at an upscale restaurant in Folsom. It always had to be upscale for him, as though an invisible documentarian were following his every move. It was important to go to the best restaurants and host the best parties. More than anything, he always had to be camera-ready.

In fairness, it was the '80s—possibly the most conspicuous-consumption decade in recent history. I was barely in my 30s and still very impressionable; he was nine years older and had it all figured out, so I didn't have to worry my little head about anything. He controlled all of the money, kept our financial records at work, and refused to answer my questions about investments. His alcoholism was the catalyst for a long, slow, fall from grace, which ended in financial ruin and a long fight with the IRS. After the divorce, I met with an IRS agent and worked out a payment plan for the six-figure debt they said we owed in back taxes. The only other option was to apply under their "innocent spouse" clause, but doing so might have dragged things out for years. They were sure I qualified, but it was a gamble. If I lost, I would owe penalties and interest for all of those years on top of what was owed on the current balance. It took twelve years of very hard work to pay them off, get my credit score back, and buy my first house.

We ordered coffee to offset the bottle of wine with lunch, and stared out the rain-streaked window without speaking.

Alone in the car on the way home from the restaurant, I thought about how far off track my life had gone in just a few short years. The nanny would be there for another two hours and I wasn't ready to go home just yet. Usually after one of our lunches, I would have her stay while I slept off the wine, before showering and getting dressed for yet another business dinner. This was happening 3-4 times a week; I added that to my list of things to worry about and deal with later. I was very good at compartmentalizing; however, I was getting migraines four or five times a month now, and I had a feeling it was all related.

The animal shelter was on the way home. We had auditioned a few dogs and kittens over the years, but they proved to be too time consuming. My daughter's preschool teachers said she was a "very active" child and had difficulty sitting still (her ADHD wouldn't be properly diagnosed for another ten years). She was struggling in preschool but seemed to calm down when it was her turn to take care of the class pet.

The barking was shrill and relentless as I stepped into the kennel area. It smelled of urine, with an after-note of dog shit and fear. I walked quickly past the dog cages and tried not to look at their pleading eyes. The quiet ones got to me—so forlorn and defeated. It was one thing to come home unannounced with a kitten, but quite another to come home with a dog.

The cattery was crowded with all colors, ages, and temperaments of cats. I bent down to get a little closer to the cages and jumped when a pair of furry arms wrapped themselves around my arm. It was a tabby with huge yellow eyes. We stared at each other for a few seconds; I was a goner. She looked like she didn't belong there, had no idea of how to get out, and I was her last chance. This cat was at least two years old. I came for a kitten.

"Looks like love to me," said the kennel worker, clearly wanting to end his shift and get home, hoping I wouldn't linger.

"I don't know," I stalled. I knew my daughter would love her, but what would my husband say? I had never done such a bold thing without asking him first.

"She's on death row. We close in 10 minutes and she's first on the list for euthanasia in the morning."

I didn't know if he was telling the truth or not, but it worked. I took her home and grinned as my child squealed with delight. We named her Pretzel, because she twisted herself up and flopped on the carpet when she was happy; she turned out to be a very happy cat. She was a sweet little Buddha and slept at the foot of my daughter's bed for many years.

She was also in the back seat of the car, next to my child, when I moved into a small rental house after the divorce. Pretzel lived for another 16 years until she died quietly of old age in her little cat bed, right around the time we got Molly and Emmy as 8-week old puppies. I called the Vet, who said to bring her in and sobbed all the way to his office. We received her cremains in a simple wooden box a few weeks later. I put the box on a shelf in the bookcase next to her framed picture. To this day, that small box is still in the same bookcase.

CHAPTER 11

OSCAR PARTY

It was a quiet drive to my daughter's house in South Lake Tahoe. While recovering from her snowboarding accident, Lyndsay said she'd had a lot of time to think about how difficult it was to have a healthy lifestyle in Hollywood. I had to take a deep breath after she told me about her decision to move to Lake Tahoe. She wanted to get out of the L.A. smog and snowboard every day. All I could do was shake my head at the thought of her getting back on that snowboard. I knew I couldn't change her mind and I was not even sure I wanted to, because I loved her fearlessness. She was right. It wasn't long after she moved to Tahoe, that she fell in love with Jeff. They had just moved in together, and we were on our way to see them in their new place.

It was a cute cottage near a busy street. Howard ended up napping during the day to shake off a stomach bug, while Lyndsay and I went shopping for a house-warming gift. They insisted on giving us the master bedroom, while they slept in the guest room with Mila, their gorgeous, red, 100-pound Husky/Malamute. Once Howard felt better, it was my turn on the couch for an afternoon of queasiness. The rest of the time we took hikes, went out for breakfast, and enjoyed the scenery from their back yard as Jeff barbequed dinner. It was going to be hard to leave, but I was very happy for my baby girl; she had found a good man.

After spending several days with Lyndsay and Jeff (and scattering more of my dad's cremains at Cave Rock, a spot overlooking the lake), we got ready to head back to Sacramento for an Oscar party at the house of my friend, Sherrye. Sherrye wanted to surprise everyone at the party, so she didn't tell them I was coming. Most of the guests were women from the book club that had been a big part of my life in Sacramento. It was a tight group, and we knew a lot about each other after years of book discussions and many, many, cases of wine. Their husbands got along well, too. There was never a shortage of parties or get-togethers with this group. I loved every one of them and struggled with the decision to leave Sacramento for Thousand Oaks, because they were important to me. They were finally going to meet my husband for the first time! I couldn't wait to introduce Howard to the women he had only heard stories about for years.

First, Howard decided that he wanted to explore Reno, 90 miles away. I was concerned about getting back in time to get cleaned-up before the party, but Howard said not to worry. We had rolled out of bed that morning without showering (again), and by the time we got back from an uninspiring trip to "the biggest little city in the world" it was too late. There was no time to shower and barely time to finish packing. I was very upset. I'd only seen my Sacramento friends once since I'd moved away and wanted to look my best at the party—not show up with dirty hair and last-night's make-up. It was bad enough that I would be underdressed, since it didn't occur to me to pack for an Oscar party. I hate feeling rushed and being unprepared, so I did the best I could with a European bath and fumed all the way to Sacramento while Howard got lost in his '50s music on satellite radio.

Of course, we were late—another pet peeve—but it didn't matter, since no one but Sherrye knew we were coming. After a not-so-grand entrance, I locked eyes with several of my former best friends. That was odd—they didn't seem surprised or happy to see me. I was disappointed and noticed that Howard was not his usual party self. He had hunkered down in front of the TV with a plate of food instead of getting to know my dearest friends. One guest, who I didn't know very well, introduced me to her mother. When the mother asked me where we lived, I told her that we didn't have a home anymore. Before I could explain about our yearlong road trip, she blurted out to the group, "They're homeless! They don't have a home!"

I could feel my face burning with embarrassment. This was not a homecoming, after all.

I was embarrassed again when Sherrye asked me where we were going to stay that night, and mumbled something about finding an RV Park. She insisted that we park in their driveway after her guests left, and gave us permission to plug Sonward into an outlet in the gazebo. It seemed like everyone at the party was surreptitiously listening to our conversation. Feeling judged, I poured myself another glass of wine and tried to suppress my disappointment and sadness.

Later that night, we went to sleep without talking about the party or anything else. The next morning, Sherrye's husband was irritated because he couldn't maneuver around Sonward in the driveway, so he had to take a different car to work. I felt like a homeless, unwelcome guest. I wanted to talk to Howard about the weird visit, but he was busy writing the first installment of his travel blog titled *The Ward*, so I let it go.

The next night was better. We stayed in their guest room and enjoyed a leisurely breakfast around the kitchen table. Perhaps, if Sherrye and I had been alone, I would have told her about how out-of-place I felt at the party. Instead, we all made small talk and promised to keep in touch before heading out the door.

CHAPTER 12

TEENAGE MARRIAGE
HOT MESS

We were both excited to get back on the road; I tried to put my feelings of alienation aside. How many times had I set myself up for disappointment because of unrealistic expectations? Did I really think that my friends would fall all over themselves when I walked through the door (yes), or that my husband would charm them the same way he had charmed me? They were all human, with moods and expectations of their own. I wanted my two worlds to love each other, but I'd been gone for several years and everyone had moved on. Because I hadn't made new friends in Thousand Oaks or in the desert, the whole thing took me by surprise. In spite of feeling displaced and more than a little hung-over the next morning, I vowed that from that point forward, my new credo would be *live in the moment, not in the past.*

We spent the day driving through another beautiful part of Northern California and decided to stop in Chico to see Bidwell Park, the third largest municipal park in California. For me, Chico was a former toxic, emotional wasteland. It had been over 40 years since the day I drove from my apartment in Davis, California, to

Chico, to confront my first-husband's girlfriend. Throughout most of the '70s, I associated Chico with abandonment and betrayal. I hadn't been back since.

We explored the downtown area, dodging students on bicycles, and later took a very long hike in Bidwell Park. I had a lot of time to think as we hiked, and it wasn't long before I found myself back in the summer of 1976.

I was 23 years old, living in Davis, California, with Barry, my then-husband of six years. I started knitting a simple 9" wide scarf the day he openly betrayed me, using a skein of yellow yarn that I found abandoned at the bottom of the linen closet. Knitting would become a way to keep my monkey-mind at bay as I wrestled with indecision.

My German mother had taught me how to knit when I was little. I used to watch her fingers dance with the yarn, knowing just when to pull and when to loop, needles clicking together with the gentle rhythm of a train. In addition to knitting, my mother also embroidered tiny flowers where holes used to be on the knees of my jeans. English was always hard for her and, many years later, rather than just crossing-out her spelling mistakes in handwritten letters to me, she turned them into elaborate trees.

My mother turned mistakes into art.

Barry and I got together in 1970, just a month after I graduated from high school, and six months before my 18th birthday. Although Barry was my brother's good friend, it wasn't until the Fourth of July, that we started talking at a party and ended up watching the sun come up while sitting on the steps of the host's apartment. Everyone else was drinking cheap beer and Boone's Farm Apple Wine, listening to Jimi Hendrix's guitar moan and scream throughout the night; we were stone-cold sober and falling in love with each other's broken parts. My #1 goal was to get the hell out of Lompoc before my soul was sucked further into the abyss of that small town. Barry had much higher aspirations, but harbored a secret, which would complicate our life in the future: he couldn't be alone, nor could he be content in a relationship as long as there was a chance that there might be someone better out there somewhere.

In other words, we were a perfect hot mess together, falling in love for all the wrong reasons.

Three months later, he asked me to marry him. The following March, we were married just two months after I turned 18. Barry joined the Air Force because he was afraid of being drafted into the Army and sent to Viet Nam. The military promised to train him as a medic, but instead decided he would make a better firefighter. After a two-day honeymoon in Santa Barbara (courtesy of Barry's parents), we were on our way to Colorado for our first assignment.

Things had not been easy from the beginning. Three months after the wedding, a drunk driver going the wrong way on the Queen Mary exit killed my 21-year old brother, Pete. The Long Beach newspaper speculated that the two cars might have actually swerved into one another at the last minute, in an attempt to avoid the collision. What if that had been true? Would my brother have survived if either of them had turned the wheel the other way? This haunted me for decades.

After seeing what remained of the car in the newspaper, I prayed that he died instantly.

The car my brother was driving was my old, red, 1964 Karmann Ghia, with the engine in the back. For some reason, this—more than the fact that it was **my** car, and I **should have** taken it with me to Colorado, instead of my dad's Mercury Marauder—made me feel partially responsible. As if the design flaw caused his death— not the huge commercial truck driven by a drunk going the wrong way onto a freeway exit at 60 mph. I felt responsible for his death, in part, because I drove a car with the trunk in the front and the engine in the back.

Barry and I were stationed at Peterson Air Force Base in Colorado Springs, Colorado. Money was extremely tight—we couldn't even afford a telephone. A police officer knocked on our door at 1:00 in the morning and asked me to call a family member for urgent information. We drove to the pay phone down the street, next to a Kentucky Fried Chicken restaurant, where I would be working in another six months. I tried to reach my parents, but there was no answer. I assumed my father had died, because he was so old (65 at the time). I called my sister in Seattle, who was too hysterical to speak. Her husband took the phone and, without any kind of preamble said, "Pete's dead." Just like that. My knees buckled and I dropped the phone.

Pete was three years older than me, and to say I idolized him would have been putting it mildly. The year before he died, he took me to my first concert to see The Doors in Santa Barbara. My father had forbidden him to take the car, so we snuck out the front door after my parents went to bed, released the parking brake, and rolled down the driveway. I was as much in awe of his friends as I was of The Doors. I remember how my brother sat next to me and pointed out different lyrics and symbolism in the music, completely at ease about having his little sister there. After the concert, we went to someone's house and everyone (except me) drank wine and talked about music. The sun peeked over the hills as we silently rolled back into my parents' driveway with the engine turned off. As far as I know, they never found out.

Years earlier, I remember watching my brother from the back seat of the family car during one of our infamous family vacations ("Six states in 5 days!" yelled my father with pride.) It was late at night and my dad insisted on making Santa Fe, because that had been his goal for the day. Pete was in the front seat smoking a Marlboro, and flicking the ashes out the wing window. Every time he did that, sparks whizzed by my back seat window. I was shocked!

He was smoking in front of my parents, and no one was stopping him!

I always thought my brother was the coolest guy on earth—still do. He had a way of unconsciously running his fingers through his hair, a habit I picked up from him. When kids at school heard I was his sister, they were impressed. He was a natural artist and writer who played guitar. Girls loved him. He clashed with my father for as long as I could remember, over all the usual things in father-son battles. However, the biggest source of my father's aggravation was Pete's shoulder-length hair (remember, it was the '60s and very early '70s). My father never missed an opportunity to ridicule my brother about his hair. I didn't know until much later that my father refused to let him come to my wedding because he wouldn't cut his hair or wear a suit. It pains me to this day.

He was buried in a suit and tie after the mortuary cut his beautiful long hair, per my dad's instructions.

I went to sleep on June 7, 1971, at the age of 18, feeling somewhat safe in the world. After Pete died on June 8, I knew better.

I was up for the rest of the night, sobbing and wondering how Barry could sleep. That was the first time I smelled a primal scent coming off my body that I would later identify as pure, unadulterated grief. You know what I am talking about if you have been through it. We left for Lompoc the next morning.

Barry had been distracted and distant throughout the long drive from Colorado Springs to Lompoc for the funeral. Just outside of Colorado Springs, he picked up a young girl who was hitchhiking. I felt stifled in my grief with a stranger asleep in the back seat. It would take us 23 hours to drive 1,200 miles to my parents' house, stopping only to fill the gas tank. I don't remember eating anything, going to the bathroom, or speaking more than a few words during the trip.

When we finally got to Lompoc, I was ragged and numb. I fell into the arms of my friends at the end of the long drive. While I stayed at home to console my grief-stricken parents, Barry took the car to visit friends and came back late, stinking of alcohol and pot. Our 3-month anniversary passed without comment, as the funeral drew near. I would never forgive him for abandoning me.

We barely made it through the funeral and the days that followed. After driving back to Colorado, we settled into a routine of separate lives; he had his work, and I dealt with the loss of my brother by putting up an impenetrable wall. Neither of us wanted to hear about the other's day.

We spent the next two years of his enlistment stationed in Colorado, until Barry had an opportunity to terminate his service early in exchange for serving double his remaining time in the Reserves (every other weekend and 2 weeks during the summer). We moved back to Lompoc and Barry attended Allan Hancock Junior College in Santa Maria, to complete his general education requirements. Junior College, as it was called then, was free in the 1970s and the GI bill paid for books. I worked full-time as a clerk at the Santa Maria substation of the Santa Barbara County Sheriff's department in order to pay the bills. There was not a lot of extra money, but I enjoyed the work and made friends easily.

Barry and I occupied very different worlds—school vs. work. We didn't talk a lot. Our marriage was failing.

You would think that after all the disappointment, disillusionment, and resentment, I would be happy to be rid of him. After years of observing my parents' stormy marriage, I believed that marriage was hard, but to give up was to fail. If we had moments of tenderness during those years, I don't remember them.

His application was accepted to UC Davis in Northern California, near Sacramento, and I'd finally come to a decision. He was a man who refused to put his arms around me if I had tears in my eyes. Knowing I had a snake phobia, he once stopped the car on a mountain road, picked up a dead snake, and slapped it across the windshield as I screamed. He held a pillow over my face in the middle of the night, and then claimed amnesia the next morning, saying I must have dreamt it. We were so wrong together. The message couldn't have been any louder. He wanted out as much as I did, but didn't want to be the bad guy, so he kept pushing me until I finally broke.

However, when I told him it was over and I wouldn't be moving to Davis with him, he was stunned. He actually broke down in tears, begging for another chance. I'd already lined up a new job at Cottage Hospital in Santa Barbara, and put a deposit down on a room in a beach house. This was going to be my fresh start in Santa Barbara. He cried, begged, and threatened suicide if I didn't move to Davis with him. I had never seen him so upset before. After several days and nights, he wore me down and we agreed to a temporary truce: I would move to Davis with him, but only if he agreed that the marriage was to be our #1 priority—our last chance. I told him I wouldn't hesitate to leave him if things didn't work out in Davis.

No sooner had we left Santa Barbara County than Barry began to act more like the old Barry. Gone was the attentive, repentant, sensitive husband. In his place was someone who was dismissive, self-absorbed, and incredibly cheap. If we stopped for a cold drink, he made a note of the cost on a 3 x 5 card. I thought it was odd, but wrote it off to the same kind of male behavior that records gas mileage; however, one month after we arrived in Davis, he presented me with a bill for 50% of all of the road trip expenses. Shit. I knew I should have moved to Santa Barbara. Why had I ignored my gut?

The apartment complex in Davis was named Ivy Towne, after the ivy-covered fences surrounding the buildings, which effectively hid the railroad tracks located within shouting distance of our living room window. The first time the 5:32 came shrieking past, I panicked and ran outside in anticipation of a horrible derailment. However, the neighbors were right. Eventually, I stopped noticing the rattling window glass, deep vibration under the carpet, and even the one-long/ four-short blasts of the air horn.

Davis was beautiful beyond anything I'd ever seen in Lompoc. I fell in love with it immediately. The campus had hundreds of trees and thousands of students on bicycles. During lunch, bands played on the quad while students threw Frisbees. I loved school and looked forward to being a student again; I couldn't wait until it was my turn. It would have been good, if only things at home had been better. Barry's miserliness and scarcity attitude extended to every corner of our daily life. He criticized the food I bought and made fun of me for suggesting an ice cream cone during one of many free street fairs we attended. I knew very little about passive-aggressive behavior and spent most of our time together trying to diffuse the constant tension.

Barry changed majors several times, because he was getting D's and F's, instead of A's and B's. His dream was to become a doctor—quite a stretch for a kid from Lompoc. I was patient for a while, but soon it became apparent that the deal we made years ago—putting him through college first before my turn—was probably not going to work. However, I loved my job on campus at the print shop. I rode my bike to work unless it was raining; then I would take one of the red double-decker buses that ran throughout Davis.

I worked on campus at the front counter of Repro Graphics. My job was to check-in print jobs from both students and professors. It was interesting work and provided contact with lots of different people. During slow times, I read every handout for a variety of college classes. Eventually, I began taking the exams, much to the delight of the professors. This is something I would repeat at American River College in Sacramento several years later. I never got below a B in this game; I just wish it had been real. This kept my loneliness at bay between 8:00-5:00, but in the evenings and on weekends, it was harder to keep my depression under control. On nights when Barry was home, he was either buried in homework, or smoking pot and drinking with friends "to relieve stress." I had to get up early every morning for work and didn't care for the taste of alcohol (this would change in the future), so I spent most nights alone, wondering how I'd gotten myself so trapped.

Part of my insecurity was, of course, immaturity. Although I'd worked for as long as I could remember, I'd never lived on my own before. I saved my babysitting money to buy my first car (the red Karmann Ghia) and was able to finish high school early by attending classes in the morning and working two part-time jobs in the afternoon during my junior and senior years. Even with all that responsibility at such a young age, I was ashamed to admit how insecure I felt about being on my own. Without life experience, and in spite of being the breadwinner of the family, I felt that Barry held my life in his hands. It was not a good feeling.

I'd long suspected that there was someone else. Probably more than one someone, but other than a constant ache in my gut, I had no hard proof. The usual signs were there: lack of eye contact, whispered phone calls that ended abruptly when I came into the room, and a new interest in clothing. The betrayal was bad enough, but for him to stray after begging for another chance was almost unbearable.

The clock was ticking on our marriage. After a while, he didn't even try to hide it anymore. He came to my work after lunch one day to let me know he was going to Chico to see his ex-girlfriend, who was a nurse and a Viet Nam veteran. His pathetic alibi was that she was going to teach him how to take blood pressure readings. How stupid did he think I was? Ironically, he cheated on her with me while she was in Viet Nam (unbeknownst to me); now he was cheating on me with her. It was a wicked, ugly circle. He correctly assumed that I wouldn't make a scene at work and graciously let me know I would have to take the bus home, because he was taking our only car.

I tried to continue working, but ended up leaving early because I couldn't hide my devastation.

I started knitting that yellow scarf around two in the afternoon. Ten hours later, I stood to roll my neck, shoulders, and arms, and decided I would put things in the hands of the universe. I made a deal with God. If Barry came home *after* 6 am, I would leave him; *before* 6 am, I would take it as a sign that I should stay.

He came home at 5:59—too close to call.

He refused to talk about what happened and accused me of an over-active imagination. It was entirely my fault. If only I trusted him, we could be happy. Why did I have to be so insecure and suspicious? We argued like this for another hour before I realized it was a waste of time. He would never tell me the truth. If I truly wanted to know, I would have to get in the car and drive to Chico to confront my husband's girlfriend.

So, I did.

Six months later, I filed for divorce and finished the yellow scarf after moving into my new apartment in Sacramento. The same day I finished the scarf, I accepted a job offer from American River College, where I would eventually meet my next ex-husband.

CHAPTER 13

MY FATHER'S GHOST

We were making our way further up the coast of Oregon as I shook off the remains of my latest stroll down memory lane and tried to focus on the positive changes in my life since retirement. Howard could be trying at times, but he'd never put me through the kind of twisted drama that my previous marriages produced.

We were on our way to Harris Beach, on the other side of the California border in Brookings, Oregon!

The last time I was at Harris Beach, I was still in elementary school. My family used to tent camp there when I was a kid. My father was a brilliant scientist, so you can imagine the kind of camper he turned out to be. I remember freezing in my little sleeping bag, feet futilely wrapped in a wool scarf for additional warmth. My brother, Pete, would chase me on the beach with huge handfuls of kelp. My older sister, Heidi, spent most of her time in the tent where she would curl her hair with extra-large, empty, orange juice cans and tap-tap-tap Chap Stick on her lips. My little brother, Tommy, was just happy to be in the middle of everyone; he had a perpetual smile and was always up for anything anyone wanted to do.

My poor mother! She had all the fun of feeding and cleaning up after us, as well as making and breaking camp (my dad was off looking at sea gulls) while we kids complained non-stop. She did everything except pack the tent. Too bad, because one year my dad forgot to pack the tent poles, so we had to tie the tent to tree branches to hold it up.

Where was *her* vacation? To this day, when I smell propane gas, I think of her boiling water for tea at the campground. Decades later, while my dad was in the hospital during his final days, he talked about Harris Beach with reverence and wonder. Some of his best memories took place there. Who knew?

We rolled into Brookings around noon and looked up two local RV campgrounds in the directory, but decided to get the lay of the land before choosing a place to stay. We had just finished driving through town when I spotted RVs through the trees. We had stumbled upon the Harris Beach State Park campground— the very campground where all those childhood memories were made in the early '60s!

After getting hooked-up ($21/night!) and visiting the clean restrooms, we headed down to the beach. I had a triple scoop of my dad's ashes in a baggie in the pocket of my cargo pants, but first— a bottle of German beer in his honor.

I forgot how cold the wind could be on the beach in Oregon. We took a paved switchback path to the water's edge. I could hear my father's ghost ("Paved path? Flush toilets?"). Camping with my dad meant we peed in the woods and risked our lives on narrow paths on the side of the cliffs. Parents didn't worry about things like kids falling off a cliff back then.

Ah, good times.

Although the sun was out, the wind was icy cold. A family with little kids and a dog gave up and headed back to the day use parking lot, leaving us completely alone on the beach. The wind was whipping my hair and I could no longer feel my ears, but I was excited about being at Harris Beach again. Just as I opened the baggie to prepare the scattering, a little old man appeared. He must have been about 90 years old with a wicked-fast stride, wearing a beret, and using a piece of driftwood as a walking stick. Howard and I silently looked at each other as he passed by.

"What would you do if he introduced himself to us with a thick German accent?" my husband wanted to know.

"That's easy; I would assume that we hadn't made it around that final curve and that we were dead."

Howard smiled and said, "I'd run."

When I first opened the baggie, the wind was brutal. However, as I shook out the contents near the water's edge, the wind died almost immediately, which meant that most of the cremains landed on the beach instead of in the water. I wrote my father's name in the sand with a rock and waited for the waves to wash away the sparkling sand that wasn't sand.

The next morning, we took a short drive into town to look for the condominium that was a second home to our good friends, Tom and Susie. Howard had worked with Tom at the courthouse for over 10 years, so when it came time for us to be married, Tom offered to perform the ceremony. We called them to let them know that we were admiring their condominium from the outside and they were delighted. Susie insisted that we have breakfast at the Oceanside Diner, a favorite of locals and tourists alike.

She was right! The Oceanside Diner is a small out-of-the-way spot filled with mostly locals. Mike, the chef ("trained at San Francisco's Culinary Academy," according to the menu), came out to take orders and bus tables during the rush. From the looks of it, every hour of every day was the rush. The diner's theme was all things NASCAR—flags, pictures, action figures of Dale Earnhardt—the works.

Large portions, ridiculously reasonable prices, and no sales tax made for a wonderful dining experience. There were about a dozen tables in the dining room, and you could tell why it was a local favorite. I felt a little self-conscious in my Dodgers t-shirt (tourist flag), although I received nothing but smiles from my fellow diners. At one point, someone's cell phone began to ring and everyone stopped eating, turned in unison, and just stared at the offender. It was a sweet older woman who quickly jumped up and took her call outside. Her table companion addressed the room, "It's okay. It's the ICU at the hospital." That seemed to satisfy the crowd, who immediately turned back to their omelets.

That wasn't the only bit of drama. Mike (the chef) exchanged angry words with a man sitting at a table in the back of the diner. The next time I looked up, the man was standing in the kitchen and Mike was yelling for him to "get out of here!" The guy grinned and loped out the door to the parking lot. Mike then ran out to the parking lot and began yelling at him again, but I couldn't make out what he was saying through the window. I love a good mystery.

In spite of the drama, you could tell that Mike was a sweetheart. After his adventure in the parking lot, he stopped by our table to make sure we were happy with the food. My eggs were especially creamy and delicious, so I asked him what he added to them to make them so good.

"Love. We make our food with love."

You have to love a guy like that; I could see myself waitressing there.

CHAPTER 14

POOPING ADVICE

Pooping: we all do it, but rarely discuss it in public (thank you). In all of my research into the RV life and road trips in general, not once did anyone discuss how one of our most basic functions might be affected by life on the road.

Sonward, our small 22' RV, actually came with a tiny toilet. However, for the sake of any future romance in the marriage, I decided early on that it would be better to use public facilities whenever possible. The only problem was that we were rarely near a clean public restroom when nature called, so either I found myself holding it in with a grimace, or suggesting that *right now* would be a good time for Howard to pull over and walk the dog before I embarrassed myself. Unfortunately, I had the additional challenge of having a shy colon when it came to public restrooms. Before we left on our road trip, I would have driven all the way home from the mall if I had to do #2. This was not an option in the middle of nowhere.

I grew up in an era where society frowned upon today's acceptance of public flatulence, ass-scratching, and general bad taste when it came to private matters. However, when you are sharing a public restroom and you only have until the gas tank finishes filling up to finish your business, you forget about a lot of your up-bringing. You also get good at masking bathroom noises. I learned that a courtesy flush or well-timed cough is usually a good mask, unless the cough itself forces new and interesting noises forth. And forget about waiting it out until everyone leaves—the other women were likely waiting for me to leave, too. So there we sat, in our little prison stalls of awkwardness.

I particularly disliked the unisex restroom inside the gas station mini mart. I always seemed to follow a big guy with a newspaper in hand, who'd eaten Thai food for dinner the night before, and washed it down with a pineapple milkshake Adding insult to injury, the toilet seat was usually up after he finished stinking up the place. What did he do, pee *afterwards*?

Once it was finally my turn, why was there always a cute guy next in line for the toilet? He would give me a look as the stench of the previous occupant wafted towards him. I wanted to explain that it wasn't me—it was the Thai-food guy before me—but I knew he wouldn't believe me. The only thing I could do was smile, hold my head up high, and gracefully walk back to the RV, hoping that there was no toilet paper stuck to the bottom of my shoe.

Let's face it—at home, there are many things you can do to preserve your dignity when it comes to bathroom habits: open a window, light a match, maybe a quick spritz of Febreze in the air. But there's no way to hide a Sheboobie snaking its way through the hose at the dump station with your husband watching and helping it make its way through.

The best advice for people who have a high need for privacy is to establish routines. Leave plenty of time in the morning for a restroom run. Be honest about having to go. Do not—repeat—do not wait for a potty emergency to share your situation. Do not hold it in, either. There is a non-negotiable window of opportunity for such things; it is better not to mess with it.

Enough said.

CHAPTER 15

SEA STACKS AND WINE

We had been on the road for a few weeks when little things began to grate on my nerves. The line between annoyance and suppressed rage began to thin with each new mile.

For example, Howard developed a habit of driving the RV as though he were pedaling a bicycle; his right foot initially pushed on the gas pedal, then he'd let up for a while to coast, then hit the gas pedal again, then coast for a while, and so on. My neck was usually sore by sundown. That's not even the worst of it! He also developed a habit of accelerating slightly before braking, causing me to step on the imaginary brake on my side of the floor and gasp, which would cause him to snap at me about startling him when I gasped. I lost 10 seconds of my life per gasp.

After Brookings, we made our way still further up the Oregon coast and eventually spent the night at the Bandon Inn ("Overlooking Old Town to the Pacific"), in Bandon, Oregon. It had been a long day with curvy roads and an icy wind. I was ravenous by the time we pulled into Bandon. Howard could go all day on just a handful of nuts and a bottle of juice, but I have to eat every few hours or I get cranky and slightly disoriented. Every day around 3:00, my blood sugar drops to an all-time low, making even simple math impossible.

It would not be a pretty afternoon in Oregon.

We stopped in Port Orford earlier that day because Howard wanted to climb a sea stack in Battle Rock Park, the site of a bizarre standoff between 9 settlers and 300 Native Americans. Sea stacks are vertical columns of rock in the sea caused by erosion through the force of the waves crashing against the rocks. Oregon is famous for them. The one in Port Orford had a path and several trees growing out of the rocks near the top.

There were many surfers in the water and a parking lot full of people with cranky kids and restless dogs. It was a steep path to the beach to reach the sea stack, and I didn't feel like making the descent with Emmy on a leash, so I stayed behind and walked her along the cliff instead. What I really wanted to do was bundle up against the wind on the deck of the Red Fish Restaurant nearby, and soak up the sun while sipping a glass of the local red wine with Emmy at my feet while Howard hiked. That's what I *should* have done, instead of pacing along the cliff. If I had, I might not have gotten so irritated when he took a short stroll on the beach afterwards, which kept me waiting even longer.

Long days on the road with lots of time for reflection had begun to highlight my relationship history of abdicating responsibility for my life because (a) I didn't like to rock the boat (b) like my mother before me, I tended to put everyone else's needs and wants over my own, (c) I found most power struggles a waste of time and/ or (d) it was usually just easier to go with the flow.

An hour after he began, he finally met me back at Sonward. With nothing more than resentment in my stomach, I smiled and pretended to listen to his story about the view from the top. I knew I had to speak my mind, or dangerously ruminate for the rest of the afternoon.

"You know what *I'd* like to do? I'd like to enjoy some local wine on the deck of that restaurant," I said, pointing to the Red Fish.

"Good idea," he answered. "Only, why don't we have some wine and a little lunch in the RV?"

Instead of holding my ground, I said okay, because I could feel an argument coming on otherwise; I was excessively wound up and more than a little hungry. Besides, what difference did it make if we ate at the Red Fish or in Sonward? We were finally going to do something I wanted to do: eat outside, share a glass of wine, and maybe work out some kinks in the itinerary.

I made lunch (we split a sandwich), cleaned up afterwards, and pouted as the wine went untouched. He was back in the driver's seat, talking about our next destination. Apparently, he had forgotten about sitting in the sun with me. I wasn't up for a long discussion or negotiation, so I begrudgingly let it go (actually, I had the argument in my head instead of out in the open). It was my retirement, too. An afternoon spent relaxing on the deck of a nice restaurant may not have been his cup of tea, but he should have done it to make me happy.

A couple of hours later, it was time to look for a place to stay for the night. After consulting the RV Park directory, we decided on the Bandon Inn less than two hours away; however, he turned off the main highway onto a small two-lane country road "to see where it would lead." What happened to the Bandon Inn? I was tired of not being consulted about detours. That half a sandwich at lunch had worn off and I needed to eat real food soon. I tried to stuff my anger and failed.

"Where are we going?" I didn't even try to hide my exasperation.

"I just saw this road and wondered where it would lead," he said.

I was hungry and angry--hangry. It probably didn't occur to him to ask me if I was up for exploring a rabbit hole in the dark on an empty stomach.

"Jesus Christ, Howard! I could chew my foot off right now—what the fuck happened to dinner and getting to Bandon before dark?"

"It'll take 5 minutes—just relax."

Forty-five minutes later, we finally turned around to find our way back to the highway.

He didn't understand why I was so upset—wasn't that what this trip was supposed to be about—exploring the road less taken? Things quickly escalated into another argument.

After walking around Bandon for another hour, we finally had a nice dinner with shitty wine at the Wheelhouse Restaurant. We were still pissed off at each other, but he was trying to rescue the evening by being cheerful, which added to my resentment. I was being a bitch and I knew it, but the day had worn me down.

That night, Howard fell asleep right away as I stared at the ceiling in the dark. The only way to get through this trip was to surrender and change my attitude; otherwise, one of us would die. I vowed to put the day behind me and start over again in the morning.

After Bandon, we stayed in a 4-star RV Park in Canyonville; visited with Howard's friends, Jim and Terry, in Roseburg; and then spent a quick night in Eugene (dinner at the Steelhead Brewery). The next day we made a surprise stop at Sea Lion Caves—our second-to-last stop in Oregon. We would be in Seattle by the weekend.

CHAPTER 16

SEA LION CAVES

When I was a kid, my family (4 kids and 2 adults in a mid-size car) would take brutally long road trips that my dad referred to as vacations. He loved the Oregon coast. I have many memories of tall trees, restless waves, cheesy tourist traps, and Sea Lion Caves. I'd been traumatized on one of our infamous family vacations while visiting Carlsbad Caverns in New Mexico. I was shocked when, a few days later, my dad pulled into the parking lot of Sea Lion Caves in Oregon. Carlsbad Caverns was a descent into hell for this 12 year old with a touch of claustrophobia; especially when they killed the lights to show how helpless we would all be if the power suddenly went out! Now I was supposed to take an elevator 200 feet through solid rock, into a cave carved by the ocean, filled with sea lions. My last memory of Sea Lion Caves ended with a power struggle between my dad and me. He thought I was being ridiculous because I didn't want to go into the elevator; I was in tears, because I was terrified.

I had not thought about Sea Lion Caves in decades, until my husband spontaneously pulled into the parking lot. We navigated our way through the gift store to the ticket window. I read the posted warnings with great interest as my husband bought our tickets. The clerk behind the ticket window could sense my rising panic and reassured me that, while earthquakes were not unheard of in the area, we would "probably" be safe. I asked a few pointed questions about the local geology (all bad news) and finally decided that I would just suck it up and try to be a good sport. I needed some currency in my marital bank account.

However, as we approached the elevator, panic began to rise in my throat. The doors opened and two people got out. I could feel Howard's hand on my back as we slowly stepped into the elevator. Just as quickly, I stepped out again.

"I'm sorry. I can't do this," I said.

"No worries—I'll see you in a while." I expected him to try to cajole me into joining him, but it was simply no big deal.

The couple who had gotten off the elevator gave me a compassionate smile. The doors closed again, as my husband and a small group of people began their descent to see the sea lions.

"Don't worry about it, honey," whispered the somewhat disheveled woman who had just gotten off the elevator with her husband.

"It took 3 Valium to get me down there."

I asked, "How was it?"

"I don't remember," was all she slurred before her husband helped her to the parking lot.

I was embarrassed and slightly ashamed that I couldn't bring myself to go with Howard, until a small, strong voice inside of me questioned why we both had to like the same things. He obviously had no problem with me bailing at the last moment. Why did I feel like there was something wrong with me because I was afraid of small places? Would I have gone there without him? Hell, no. Was I letting him down? Yes, maybe a little. Could I live with that? Yup—I could.

Howard came back to the RV full of stories about the caves. He wasn't the least bit mad at me for staying behind, and even got a refund for my ticket from the sadist at the ticket counter.

Our next stop was the Tillamook Cheese Factory in (where else?) Tillamook, Oregon. This was definitely more my speed.

CHAPTER 17
OLYMPIC NATIONAL PARK

S oon we crossed over the Astoria Bridge that spans the Columbia River between Oregon and Washington. It's the last completed segment of Highway 101 between Olympia, Washington, and Los Angeles, California. It is also the longest continuous truss bridge in North America and high off the water, which gave Howard a slight case of the yips. It also got to me, because it was over 4 miles long and took forever to get to the other side. Still, we were happy to be in a new state and looking forward to a visit with our good friend, Karen, as well as my sister, Heidi. First, a brief stop in the Olympic National Park to see the Hoh Rain Forest.

The first thing Emily did after we reached at the Visitor Center was take a huge crap on the sidewalk, horrifying several tourists. Howard had gone inside to get a trail map and, of course, he was the one with the poop bags, so I stood guard over Emmy's doody and smiled at people who gave me the stink-eye until he came out.

The plan was to take a 90-minute hike to see the wonders of the rain forest up close and personal, but I lost interest after it started raining. The road to get there was rough and it took a lot longer than expected; plus, I had the start of a bladder infection and didn't want to be too far away from a bathroom. I asked Howard to go without me.

In all honesty—I needed a change of scenery. Appreciating nature was losing its charm. It's one thing to see breathless vistas, towering redwoods, and awe-inspiring canyons, while on a two-week vacation. It is quite another, after weeks of dragging my sorry ass out of bed in the morning to walk through the fog in my sweat pants to use the public restroom. I needed some pampering for my spirit, as well as my aching back. Our cramped quarters made my job of folding the bedding every morning difficult. Driving several hundred miles each day further aggravated the compressed disks, arthritis, and bone spurs in my lower back.

With apologies to Carlos Santana, "my thoughts were dark and my house was cold," when Howard took off on his hike alone.

Then I remembered my vow: this is where I'd planted my flag. It hit me how much I loved this man! As though reading my mind, he came back to make sure I was okay and to give me the keys to the RV to run the heat in case I got cold while he was gone. After a quick kiss, he was off again.

I drank the last of the Hogue Chardonnay that we bought outside of Tillamook and ate salty, white corn tortilla chips, while listening to Andrea Bocelli on my headphones.

I would have been miserable on that hike.

CHAPTER 18

SEABROOK

We pushed on to one of my bucket list destinations: Pacific Beach, Washington—home of Seabrook. When I lived in Sacramento, I worked 60-hour weeks filled with chaotic business trips, endless meetings, exhausting conferences, and numerous conventions throughout the United States. I was burning precious years off my life, and dreamed of the day I could walk away from it all and live peacefully in my little cottage by the sea. One day, I got an email promoting a place called Seabrook, a planned community (beach village) on the coast of Washington state. I immediately signed up to receive updates. After construction was completed, I fantasized about living there amongst the redwoods and the beach. Someone had broken ground on my retirement dream! I pinned the brochure to the bulletin board above my desk and stared at it during long conference calls. I thought that if I saved my bonus checks and sold my house in a decent market, I could probably retire there in another ten years or so.

There was still plenty of daylight left when Howard and I pulled into Seabrook for the night. We walked around the quaint town square, browsed inside *The Salty Dog* (a very cool shop which specialized in all-things-dog), and smiled when the owner invited us to a "Yappy Hour" for dog owners and their pooches. Emily and I had a new friend. Next, we toured the beautiful model homes. I could see myself living there, but I couldn't see the two of us living there. I was a moody writer, prone to long periods of isolation (perfect for this small coastal community), while my husband thrived on new experiences in places with a downtown. Rather than feeling disappointed, I was encouraged that I could evaluate Seabrook objectively. It just was not going to work for us, so I crossed it off the list of potential hometowns.

It would have saved countless hours of anxiety, if only I'd known about our post-trip hometown in advance.

The next morning, we woke up to thick fog and hundreds of people fading into the distance on the beach. They were bundled up against the cold, clutching clam rakes. It was razor clam season, and everyone was trying to catch his or her limit. The beach was eerily quiet, in spite of the crowd.

A few hours later, we drove onto the Kingston- Edmonds ferry to Seattle to spend one night with our good friend, Karen, in Duvall, Washington. She insisted on giving us her bedroom and told us to relax when Emmy chased her two cats up the stairs of her condominium. She was half-right. Within hours, Emmy was asleep on the couch; one of the cats was asleep on the back of the couch; and the other cat hid under the bed and scowled. Not only did she give up her bedroom, but Karen also had a gift basket with chocolates and trashy gossip magazines waiting (and lots of wine in the refrigerator). She cooked plank-salmon, shared thousands of pictures from her recent trip to Italy, and didn't mind when I passed out on the couch next to Emmy. One night was not enough, so we promised to stop by again after visiting my sister in Seattle.

CHAPTER 19
FLASHBACK TO GERMANY

When I was a kid, my father worked in the aerospace division of the Boeing Company in Seattle—still considered "the heart of modern aviation and space travel." We moved from where I was born in Germany, to Victoria, British Columbia, to Seattle, Washington. I still remember being woken-up in the middle of the night in our little house in the country in Germany. My mother told me to hurry and get dressed because we were leaving. She said I could bring any toy I wanted, but only one. I chose the book she read to me before bed every night. I was not quite five years old, a native speaker of German, and had never been outside of Munich in my short life. We were about to spend three weeks aboard an ocean liner called the *Arosa Star*, crossing the Atlantic during hurricane season, en route to Montreal, Canada, where we would take a train to our new home in Victoria, British Columbia. Two years later, we would take the ferry from Victoria to Vancouver, and drive from Vancouver to Seattle (smuggling our cat, Mitzi, across the border under the front seat), for my dad's new job at Boeing.

I was thinking about the early years on the way to Seattle, and it made me wonder how much of an affect my family's secrecy had on my hard-wiring when it came to trust.

We left Germany under cover of night. During the long trip across the Atlantic, and during the first few months in Canada, my father told us not to speak to anyone or answer questions beyond our first names. *No one was to be trusted.* I didn't know that my scientist father had been forced to work on the V2 missile during the war in a place called Peenemunde. He, Werner von Braun, and other German scientists, designed experimental rockets, which regularly blew up until they figured out what was wrong with the trajectory—under penalty of death, if they continued to get it wrong. However, they were also secretly working on another project that the rest of Germany knew nothing about: rockets that could reach the moon.

Although the war ended 7 years before I was born, my father still believed that his name was on a list of scientists who would never be allowed to leave Germany alive, and he took no chances. That might explain why we lived without neighbors in the isolated and rural village of Strasslach, Germany, or why we had a fierce German Shepherd for a watchdog, who allowed no one except my father close enough to feed him. After the ban on talking to strangers was lifted, I was still hesitant to trust grown-ups. Even making friends was confusing, because I couldn't get out of secrecy-mode.

According to my parents, everything, and everyone, was dangerous; vigilance was critical for survival.

After five years at Boeing, my father got a call from Werner von Braun, asking him to come to Huntsville, Alabama, to help fulfill President Kennedy's goal of "putting a man on the moon and returning him safely before the end of the decade." My father accepted the challenge and we moved again.

CHAPTER 20
SEATTLE SISTER

My sister and I are five years apart in age (I am younger). Heidi eloped when she was 18 to escape Huntsville, Alabama, as well as the stress of living in a house filled with bickering on a good day, and horrible arguments that would last forever, on a bad day. I felt as if someone had ripped off my right arm when she left, even though we fought like—well, like sisters. It was not until we were both divorced that we truly reconnected and began spending a lot more time together. I lived in Sacramento and she lived in Seattle, so we took turns flying back and forth.

However, they were more than just visits—we always planned fun things to do. Once, we went to a resort on Lake Tahoe for a long weekend. Another time, I enrolled us in a "High Tea" class from which we were almost thrown out over a slight misunderstanding involving a small blowtorch. I might have misused it while finishing off our homemade lemon meringue petit fours. We walked on the beach at Half Moon Bay, went to a Fisherman's Festival in Bodega Bay, and saw many movies together. We understood each other and laughed at the same things; her killer dry wit made me wet my pants on more than one occasion. Once I met Howard, our visits grew further apart. We were long overdue for a good sit-down by the time we rolled into Seattle.

Heidi's son, Jason, used his day off to give us a tour of the area. First, we drove downtown for a peek at the Space Needle. Next, we parked the car and walked to the wharf for a bowl of clam chowder at Ivar's Restaurant; then over to Alki Point on Elliott Bay, for a beautiful view of the Seattle skyline; and finally, dinner with the rest of the family, including Heidi's daughter and granddaughter, Jennifer, and Lauren. Howard and I reserved a room for my sister in our hotel so we wouldn't lose valuable time commuting back and forth from her place in the suburbs. It had been a full day, and we were all tired by the time the three of us got back to the hotel.

The next morning, Howard wanted to see Buddy Holly's original tour bus, which was on display in the parking lot of the XXX Rootbeer Drive-in in Issaquah. After a quick breakfast at the hotel, we were on our way to see the bus. First, a quick stop to pay our respects at Jimi Hendrix's grave at the Greenwood Memorial Park in Renton.

After taking pictures of the tour bus, we ate lunch at the XXX Rootbeer Diner. It was hard to leave, not knowing how long it would be until I saw my sister again. We were never alone long enough to catch up on each other's lives; I wondered briefly if I should make plans to come alone next time. One of my goals on this trip was to clarify my core values. I wanted to be much better at keeping in touch with what was left of my family.

After a long good-bye (and a few tears), Howard, Emmy, and I, hit the road again for a return visit to Karen on our way east.

CHAPTER 21
WINTER STORM WARNING

O ne of the challenges of being on the road is maintenance. It is easy to find a place to change the oil in the car, but not so easy when it comes to finding a salon for a root touch-up for my hair. I have seen some beautiful women with silver hair, but I am not one of them. I saw my first silver hair in my early 50s, and have been maintaining my blonde hair ever since. When people ask me if this is my natural color, I give them an honest answer. "Of course this is my natural color—back when I was seven years old."

We no longer live in a "does she or doesn't she?" world, so when I complained to Karen about being overdue for a root touch-up during our second visit, she suggested that I come with her the next day. Miss Karen was also enhancing what nature gave her, and offered to call her hair lady and get me in at the same time.

But, noooooooo. Mr. Wonderful had itchy feet to get back on the road. I was not looking forward to leaving our comfortable bed at Karen's home—not to mention her hot shower, adult-size toilet, and girlfriend-time. Karen and I shared a lot of laughter and drank our fill of wine; I didn't want to leave. Howard didn't share our love of wine and being the only sober one in the room got old fast.

We pushed on in spite of my silver roots and the threat of a winter storm warning.

I respect snow in the same way that I respect the ocean—both require vigilance. I wasn't the best passenger in the world under normal conditions, but if given a choice between waiting out a blizzard or driving in it, I would take the waiting-out option every time. Besides, had we turned around when the flakes began to fall, I would have made that hair appointment with Karen. Howard, however, was not going to let a little weather delay our road trip—especially at the prospect of more girl-talk and bottomless bottles of wine.

It didn't take long before I noticed how few cars there were on the road, with even fewer coming from the opposite direction. Had they closed the pass on the Spokane end? Were we going to be stranded with only ¼ of a tank of gas? The generator to heat the RV won't turn on if the gauge falls below ¼ tank. Where was the Highway Patrol, in case we needed an escort off the mountain?

The longer we drove in the blizzard, the higher my anxiety level rose. A few years earlier, I became stranded in a blizzard while driving home from my friend's place in Lake Tahoe. Not only was it scary as hell when visibility got down to zero, but it was also cold by the side of the road with the car turned off. The snowplows finally arrived, along with a CHP escort. Normally a two-hour trip, it ended up taking me well over 6 hours to get home.

I glanced down at the speedometer and noticed we were doing 55 mph. No big deal in clear visibility, but neither of us could see beyond the hood of the car. Shit.

I white-knuckled it for as long as I could, before slowly pulling my camera out of the bag and snapping a few pictures through the windshield; I told Howard I was gathering proof for the jury that would <u>not</u> convict me for what I was planning to do to him if we survived. He was not amused. After much tension and a few tears, we finally made it over the mountain pass and into the sunshine of

Spokane, where we took a very long walk on the beautiful Gonzaga University campus to unwind.

Continuing east from Spokane, we crossed the Washington-Idaho border. Things were much better on the drive along Interstate 90. We even squeezed in a side trip to Lake Coeur d'Alene, one of the top five lakes in the world, according to National Geographic. We celebrated St. Patrick's Day with a stop at the throwback little mining town of Wallace, Idaho, before finally settling in for the night in Missoula, Montana.

Whew!

The next day brought another mountain-blizzard adventure. We made it as far as the first exit on the edge of Butte, Montana, and found an okay- hotel room for the night—that turned into three nights, after they closed the highway. Fortunately, for Howard, there was a series of golf tournaments on TV. The next day, I made a few phone calls and got an appointment for a root touch-up at JC Penny, the only salon within walking distance of our hotel.

I came home an odd shade of blonde, because the stylist said she didn't know how to touch up only the roots. I believe her exact words were, "They don't test for that in Montana—you must be from California." I was desperate, so I let her color my hair from the roots to the tips. Oh, and she "trimmed" my bangs and cut them a little further back on my head, saying they were "kind of uneven." I came back to the hotel room looking like the kid on a can of Dutch Boy Paint. Howard had no comment—smart guy.

I spent the rest of the day mumbling about how we could have stayed in Duvall with Karen, instead of spending three days at the Best Western in Butte-fucking-Montana. The golf tournament must have been interesting, because Howard acted as if he had not heard a word I said.

The sun finally came out and we pressed on …

CHAPTER 22

ON THE ROAD TO SOMEWHERE IN THE MIDDLE OF NOWHERE

I t was an awful fight.

As we were ambling down yet another long stretch of highway, I pulled out my laptop and put on head phones to listen to Kenny Chesney sing about feeling peaceful in the Caribbean. I love writing with music in the background, but it was hard to write that day because Howard kept talking to me, pointing out Dairy Queens and RV dealerships, as we drove through small communities. He would sometimes get weird when I was on my laptop, and try to distract me by being talkative. For the record, he says that it was just his way of trying to engage me in conversation.

I was in the middle of writing a profile of where I would like to live after the trip. My fantasy included a town with mostly sun, enough rain, the odd snowstorm, and beautiful fall colors. It would also have a Target, and maybe even a Whole Foods store. There would be a quaint wine bar with special events a couple of nights a month. It would be easy to find a book club, a hair salon, and a massage therapist. Dogs would be welcome almost everywhere. You could buy season tickets for concerts, speaker series, and plays. Ideally, there would be a large airport nearby, as well as proximity to the ocean. It would be a small town near a big city, possibly a college town. We would be proud to invite our children and friends for a visit. Housing would be affordable, but still a bit of a stretch. I would be able to create the home I wanted, with very little clutter and lots of natural light; a small backyard with just enough room for a few trees and an herb garden; candles throughout the house; and beautiful dishes on which to serve healthy gourmet dinners.

We'd been talking about where to live when the road trip was over, but had different approaches to finding a new home. I focused on the characteristics of the community, while Howard was more comfortable leaving it open-ended. He felt we would know when it was right, while my experience told me that research and creating a profile was critical. No one was right or wrong—we just had a different way of getting there. These discussions usually got us nowhere; we got lost in the process. I would usually shake my head, give up, and stew for a while.

As the miles rolled on, my stewing turned global. I remembered the first time he began talking about the trip while we were still dating; I said it sounded like fun (I was being polite). What it *really* sounded like was a marathon race to this non-runner. Before I met Howard, I'd experienced that life to a small extent in a 28' luxury RV with all the bells and whistles, and it just was not my cup of tea. I hated the sheer footprint of that gas-guzzling beast and the way cars blew by us when the mountain road finally opened up a passing lane. Sonward was smaller and much more efficient, which was good for the environment, but bad for my back.

I didn't think the trip was a good idea from the start, but I was sure that if I told the truth, he would go without me. At the time, a one-year separation would have been a deal-breaker for the relationship. When he talked about a year on the road, I tried to stay neutral, even downright supportive at times, never really believing he would buy an RV. Yet, he did. Once Sonward was part of the family, there was no backing out—I would have to make the best of it.

It was encouraging at first. I enjoyed our short trips before retirement, as well as the first part of our longer trip. However, after a while, the small living space, lack of storage, teeny-tiny bathroom, irregular schedule, and killer potholes, really began to grate on me. In fairness, Howard made sure we stayed in hotels regularly to break up the trip. He knew it was his dream, not mine, and tried to make sure I was comfortable. But after a few months, he was tired of hearing my complaints, and I was tired of being ignored.

I wish I could go back in time and be a better partner by speaking up instead of clamming up. I thought I was avoiding arguments but instead, I was building up resentment.

We had a horrible argument shortly after our second anniversary. I was in a very bad mood after discovering a rash on my foot from a questionable shower floor. I was also dealing with yet another bladder infection. After hours of silence, I finally snapped.

"Howard, how can you pretend that everything's fine?" That came out a lot louder than I meant.

Now it was his turn to snap.

"Here we go—what now, Sonja? Are you going to tell me again how I fucked-up some small part of your day? I can't seem to do anything right, but not you—you're never wrong. You're also never happy. Why should I even try?"

At least he was talking. I tried to explain how frustrating it was not to be able to vent occasionally, but I couldn't get a full sentence out. Apparently, I was not the only one holding on to resentment. Howard finally blurted out the truth.

"Do you know how long I've waited to do this trip?" he asked.

"I thought this was *our* trip, or at the very least—"

"Well, guess what, Sonja? You're wrong—big shock! This is *my* trip and *you are ruining it for me.*"

Now it was my turn for righteous indignation.

"THAT IS SUCH BULLSHIT! When is it going to be my turn to do what I want, instead of hiking over another fucking pile of rocks in the middle of nowhere?"

"Why don't you have another glass of wine," he said, with a sarcastic smirk.

"I'd love to! That's the only thing that keeps me from jumping in front of the next semi!"

"That's it. This is not working. Maybe we should think about Plan B, and I'll finish this trip alone."

Just like that, the argument was over—my husband wanted to abandon me in the middle of the country with no home, no job, no transportation, and a wicked bladder infection. "Plan B," whatever that was, was not an option. We were stuck with one another.

CHAPTER 23

HIGH IN COLORADO

We ignored each other for the next two days. As usual, Howard snapped back first and pretended nothing had happened between us; he was his usual cheerful self. No apology, no tying up loose ends, no checking in to see how I was doing. I was beginning to hate us. Then we got some good news.

Howard's daughter and her husband called to say that they were expecting their first baby. He was over the moon with happiness and I couldn't stain that moment for him with my attitude, so I lightened up. We decided to go to Austin, Texas, to see the happy couple and vowed to enjoy the stops along the way. It worked.

Arches National Park, near Moab, Utah, should be on everyone's bucket list for the stunning scenery, great hiking trails, and awe-inspiring views of unusual rock formations. We both loved the challenge of hiking to the iconic Delicate Arch, a 65-foot tall freestanding natural arch, which also appears on Utah license plates. It was a hot day and we were exhausted by the time we finished our 7-mile hike up the side of a mountain, but agreed that it was worth it after we finally reached the Arch. We high-fived each other before beginning the long descent back to the parking lot.

Next stop: Cortez, Colorado. We stopped to stretch our legs and, as luck would have it, stumbled upon a high school baseball game in progress. After watching for a while and cheering for the underdog, we ate a hot dog and drank a Coke before taking Emmy for a walk at the community park next door, where she discovered a new favorite treat: goose poop! Howard dragged an unwilling Emily back to Sonward and away from the allure of the goose poop. We spent the next several days trying to avoid her breath.

Later, we got lucky again in southwest Colorado where we discovered the Mesa Verde National Park—home to ancient pueblos and petroglyphs.

Finally, after several long days in the sun, we found ourselves in a cool little bar in Durango, listening to two old guys play the blues on acoustic guitars.

We were going with the flow and holding hands again.

We spent a peaceful night in a great former mining town in Ouray, Colorado, named after Chief Ouray, a great Ute Indian Chief. The town's nickname is "The Switzerland of America," because of its setting at the narrow head of a valley, surrounded by steep mountains. All of Main Street is a National Historic District! It is beautiful, historic, and quaint, all at the same time.

It's also home to "The Million Dollar Highway," aka Highway 550. The drive was gasp-worthy, with 1,000-foot drops to certain death, due to a lack of guardrails. However, I had learned my lesson during the blizzard and made jokes instead of freaking-out. Besides, Highway 550 is part of the San Juan Scenic Byway and Skyway, truly one of the most beautiful drives we had ever taken. Next time, we will spend more time in town and soak in the hot springs.

Howard and Emmy took another long walk at sunset while I unpacked at our hotel, The Ouray Victorian Inn. We were treating ourselves to a nice dinner, long soak in the tub, and getting caught-up on the latest episodes of *Breaking Bad* and *The Amazing Race*. We had reached an unspoken agreement that we would both try harder.

We had no idea what Mother Nature would soon have in store for us.

CHAPTER 24

WIND, WIND, AND MORE WIND

I t is amazing how different the world looks after a good night's sleep. After leaving Ouray, we crossed the Great Divide (11,300 ft. elevation) and eventually saw a sign for Royal Gorge, the highest suspension bridge in America. Howard immediately said he wanted to check it out. The only problem was the wind; it was blowing at close to 40 mph, with 70 mph gusts. We had a brief discussion and decided to check it out anyway; if it weren't safe, surely they wouldn't let anyone on the bridge.

They closed the bridge because it wasn't safe.

Once back on the highway, Howard said, "I don't want to freak you out, but look ahead."

"Ohhhhh, shit …," I said softly.

A huge dust storm was quickly approaching from the north, blowing across the highway, obliterating the line between the road and the sky, dwarfing cars unfortunate enough to be in its path. I braced myself, but driving through it was much less dramatic than watching it from a distance. Disaster averted.

We found a wonderful RV Park near Pueblo and, after walking Emmy, and doing a few loads of laundry, we settled in for a quiet night. The wind was still bad, but we felt safe. We planned to have an early night after a very long day.

No sooner had we turned out the lights, when the RV started rocking as the wind picked up speed again. You couldn't hear it while we were driving, but now that we were stationery, it howled, moaned, and swirled, underneath the floor boards, through cracks in the seals of the window, and over the air conditioning unit and satellite dish on the roof. It was so bad, that at one point we got on the Internet to see what was going on in nearby towns. Monarch Pass had 91 mph gusts! Sleep was out of the question. We kept the lights on and kept checking online to track the path of the wind-storm. Eventually, we got somewhat used to it and became drowsy. I dozed off thinking about the poor people in the tent a few sites away. If things got worse, they could always sleep in the restroom.

Speaking of the restroom, the timing could not have been worse, but I had no choice—the storm scared the—well, it scared me in many ways. I had to go, and I was *not* going to do it in the RV. You should have seen Howard's face when I told him I was going to brave the elements and run to the restroom. He insisted on walking me to the bathroom a hundred feet away, and waited patiently until I was done. I kept yelling, "are you still out there?" to make sure he had not been blown away by the wind. Our little field trip in the middle of the night turned out to be a good thing, because on the way back (bracing ourselves against the wind, pausing between large steps as though we were characters in a crazy opera) we had a chance to see how far away the nearest tree was from where we were parked. Nothing was going to fall on us that night. Even though it was after 1:00 am, there were many lights on in sites around us—we weren't the only ones awake. Sleep finally came sometime after the last online weather-check around 3:00 am.

We survived the night! The next morning found us singing along with Elton John's *Tumbleweed Connection* album in its entirety and streaking towards New Mexico for two days at the Santa Fe Inn and Spa—complete with rainfall showerheads and a massage appointment! There was a casino near the resort, restaurant options, and no wind.

Santa Fe, here we come—we had earned it.

CHAPTER 25

SANTA FE, NEW MEXICO

I had not been back to Santa Fe since my good Sacramento friend Linda and I spent a few days there when she was considering buying a second home. I distinctly remember feeling peaceful, even though Santa Fe is in the high desert and a plane ride away from the ocean. Maybe it was because Santa Fe is an art-based community with more art galleries per capita than New York City, or perhaps the abundance of spiritual retreats had whispered to my soul.

As an artist, Linda had the inside scoop on the city. She dragged me to small, elegant showrooms, as well as huge, dusty warehouses filled to the rafters with paintings and sculptures for sale. She was looking for inspiration and also wanted to gauge whether or not her paintings would be of interest to gallery owners (they were). However, her #1 priority was to look for a small studio she could use as a second home where she could paint without the distractions of her busy life as an interior designer in Sacramento. We ate well, drank in moderation, and flirted with the locals. We went to a very trendy bar one night, dressed to the nines, and wondered why none of the men flirted back. The bartender overheard our conversation and told us the history of the gay bar in which we were enjoying our Martinis. He bought our next round and tried not to laugh as we contemplated our next move.

Ten years later, I was back.

After Howard and I got Emmy settled into our hotel room, we took a long walk through the city. The drama of the wind the night before seemed to have brought us closer together; I was in a sanguine mood, anxious to create new memories. Of course, it helped that I was only hours away from a 90-minute massage, thanks to Mr. Wonderful. First, we took a very long walk, followed by a narrated tram ride through Canyon Road, a winding road through beautiful and historic adobe homes. Although I was fascinated by the history, and stunned by the beauty of Santa Fe, I was ready for my massage and couldn't wait to get back to the hotel.

Soon I was on a heated massage table in a dark room with the sound of soft Native American flutes playing in the background, and enjoying the first massage of our road trip. I could feel my mind unspooling with the gentle kneading of my rock-hard lower back. It didn't take long for my imagination to take over and, as usual, a series of seemingly random thoughts led to thoughts of home again.

I wanted to start fresh with all new kitchen essentials, table linens, new sheets, and a small closet full of clothes that both fit, and felt great.

I thought about my friend in Sacramento whose house burned down and, rather than mourn her loss ("they were just things,") she was grateful for the safety of her family and saw the fire as a chance to create a new home filled *just with things they loved or used regularly*—no clutter from the past. Her clutter had literally gone up in smoke.

This led to thoughts of self-care. I have very rarely spent a lot of money on myself, beyond the occasional massage for my train-wreck of a back. One exception happened shortly before my daughter moved away for college. I had saved for us to go to Hawaii for her birthday but, at the last minute, she was unable to get time off from her new job. I didn't really want to go without her, so I took advantage of the trip insurance for a full refund. After determining a very conservative estimate of what we would have spent in Hawaii ($250/day), I decided I would still take the time off. Instead of going to Hawaii, I stayed home and spent $250 a day on any damn thing I wanted without guilt. I slept in, went to nice restaurants for lunch and dinner, shopped less than you would have thought, and bought tickets to future plays and concerts. I don't regret a dime of it to this day. It was money well spent.

Money and financial freedom/solvency used to make me feel secure, but never so much so that I could justify wasting money. I banked the majority of my paycheck after paying my bills, and 100% of my bonus checks. Rather than drive a luxury car, I was able to pay for my daughter's college education without either of us going into debt. I was also able to pay my bills in full each month and save for the future. When I finally got to the point of buying my own house in Sacramento, I felt like a successful grown-up at last. Finally, I lived where and how I wanted. I was free to create my simple, yet beautiful home. Peace at last--no one could take that away from me.

No wonder I felt so anxious and out of control on the road; I no longer had an income. I was more fortunate than many, with a small 401k and a savings account for emergencies, but I was now financially dependent on my husband--something I swore I would never, ever, in a million years, do.

My thoughts were straying into the stress zone, so I tried to refocus. I couldn't help thinking about my hard-earned first house in Sacramento.

As the massage therapist was working on my feet, I thought about how I used to spend hours wandering around the outdoor section of Home Depot, looking for small touches for my back yard. I would usually pick up a wind chime, bird feeder, or glazed pot, if they were on sale. Making a home for my daughter and me had spiritual significance.

This led to memories of our life in apartments before I bought the house. When Lyndsay was still in middle school, we lived in a small two-bedroom apartment in a beautiful complex called Somerset Hills. I chose it because, among other things, there were waterfalls throughout the complex, which sounded like the ocean at night through my open window. The Cape Cod style buildings were lush with landscaping and a small walking trail. Outside my apartment, Camellia hedges grew in the shade and Bougainvillea plants climbed up trellises in the sun. The complex was near my daughter's school, a great grocery store, and the best Sushi place in the world. There was a killer barbeque joint nearby, as well as a Chinese restaurant within walking distance, which specialized in homemade War Won Ton soup that would knock the socks off any cold or flu.

Our unit had its own small patio in the back—perfect for a chaise lounge, large umbrella, small table, and many container plants; my little reading nook. Although I rarely used the pool, spa, or clubhouse, it was nice to know they were there. I have very fond memories of cleaning our place every Saturday, putting away a week's worth of groceries, folding the last of the laundry, paying bills, and enjoying the smell of a roast in the oven. It didn't get much better than that.

I only wish I had known at the time that this was what *true abundance* looked like, instead of constantly worrying about money. When I had money, I worried about somehow losing it. When I didn't have it, I worried about how I would get it. My scarcity attitude held me hostage through some of the best times of my life.

After the massage was over, I relaxed on a chaise lounge near a waterfall by the courtyard pool, wrapped in a comfortable white spa robe, and sipping on ice water with cucumbers floating in the glass. I reflected on how good my life had been; how many times

I had had most of what I wanted, and all of what I needed. I saw with clarity how I had allowed fear to take center stage. Instead of enjoying what I had, I obsessed about what was missing, or what could go wrong.

Is that what I was doing on this trip, too? What would happen if I stopped being vigilant?

Even Atlas shrugged, eventually.

CHAPTER 26

CO-INCIDENCE OR MYSTERY?

W e didn't argue or bicker once the entire time we were in Santa Fe. I was finally in my element, doing the things I wanted to do. Either we were getting better at compromising, or knowing a massage was waiting for me made it easier to be a good sport.

We both enjoyed watching Emmy, stretched out in the sun on the balcony of our hotel room amid the potted Bougainvillea. Although I struggled daily with the confinement and physical discomfort of our small RV, Emmy never indicated any sort of problem, in spite of being much older than I am in dog years. I made a mental note to take a lesson. She gave us one of her million dollar Golden Retriever smiles after we got back to the hotel room. It took her a little longer to get up than usual.

After two tranquil days in Santa Fe, we were once again back on the road and on our way to Clovis, New Mexico: home of the Norman and Vi Petty Museum and Recording Studio. We almost missed it, because it was in a non-descript building on an average street. Howard was in his element! He is a huge Buddy Holly fan, and the trip to Clovis turned into a rock and roll pilgrimage to see the studio where Holly and other artists such as Roy Orbison, Buddy Knox, Waylon Jennings, and Bobby Vee recorded their hits.

I loved the vintage soda-shop vibe, replicating the 1950s. I finished looking at everything in about 45 minutes. Meanwhile, Howard was still at the first exhibit: an exact replica of Petty's recording studio. I knew he would be there for a while, so I told him I would wait for him in Sonward. It was a hot day in Clovis, and we had parked illegally, taking up two spots. Instead of running the noisy generator for the air conditioner, we pulled down the window shades, turned on the rooftop fan to keep air circulating, and opened the windows for Emmy. It was much cooler inside than outside, but I still didn't like her to be in the RV under those conditions. I kissed my husband, walked two blocks back to Sonward, and read my Kindle until a lazy afternoon nap took over. Two hours later, a grinning Howard was ready for our next pit stop: Lubbock, Texas!

We had a Twilight Zone experience in Lubbock, but before I tell you about it, you should know that Howard is a scientist at heart (unless it concerns his beloved Yankees—don't you dare jinx them). Over the years, we have had countless conversations about spirituality, the existence of a soul, life after death, synchronicity, and what some people would consider other "woo-woo" topics. He has an open mind about things outside of his belief system, but is sure that once you are dead, you are dead.

On the other hand, I believe that there are still great mysteries.

There is a scene in the movie, *Contact*, in which Jodi Foster (the scientist) and Mathew McConaughey (self-proclaimed "Man of God") are having a conversation. Jodi Foster's character says she does not believe in anything without proof.

Mathew McConaughey asks her if she loved her father.

Jodi Foster's character lost her father when she was a young girl. She replied, "Of course."

Mathew McConaughey's character says, "Prove it."

I agree with Albert Einstein: Not everything that can be count-ed counts and not everything that counts can be counted. My gut tells me that when someone dies, his or her spirit lives on. Whether it manifests itself in the hearts and memories of people who loved them, or just outside my field of vision, form does not matter to me.

After a very long drive, we finally reached Lubbock late in the afternoon, but had a hard time finding the City of Lubbock Cemetery. Our GPS had us scurrying through neighborhoods and down dead-end streets as we raced against the clock. The sun was going down as we turned off the GPS and just looked for signs in the general vicinity of where it was supposed to be. *Voila!* We stumbled upon it.

We couldn't find the main entrance to the cemetery. Eventually, we found a locked gate at a narrow side entrance. We turned around to leave, when all of a sudden, a Buddy Holly song called, *It Doesn't Matter Any More,* came on the satellite radio station. I was busy looking up the hours of the cemetery on my laptop for a return visit the next day, and didn't notice the coincidence until Howard got a funny look on his face and said, "I'm not sure, but I have a feeling we're supposed to be here." That's when we heard the gate opening! A car from the other side of the fence was ex-iting, which triggered the gate. It also triggered my husband to throw Sonward in reverse and burn rubber to get through the gate before it closed again.

This wouldn't be the first time we had a "voice from beyond" make itself known. It started years ago, when I began finding pen-nies in odd places after my mother died. I found three on her birthday! One was on the floor of the cab I took to the airport in Austin, Texas. I noticed another in the crosswalk while I was wait-ing for the light to change after landing in Burbank, California. I found the third penny in my suitcase, as I was unpacking after I got home. I began to think of the pennies as my mom's way of saying Hi ("pennies from heaven"). More than once, I found a penny after storming out of the house for a cool-down walk around the block.

Do I believe my deceased mother physically placed pennies in my path to stay in touch? No. However, when I stop what I am doing to pick up a penny and smile in remembrance of my mother, is she alive in my heart? Absolutely.

Still ... what are the odds of finding *three* pennies in *two* different states on her birthday? What are the odds of a Buddy Holly song coming on satellite radio, just as a car exits the cemetery in which he is interred, allowing us to illegally enter and pay tribute after closing time?

Coincidence or mystery?

CHAPTER 27

THE BLAME GAME

We were on our way to Austin, Texas, to see Howard's newly pregnant daughter and husband when one of us said something stupid, and the other reacted with sarcasm. This led to a discussion of how sarcasm is disrespectful, which led to a discussion about disrespectful behavior taking on many forms, etc., etc., etc.

For the next five hours, the trip was eerily quiet, each of us stewing in our own righteousness, or filled with old accusations and denials. How could we have been so close only days ago? It really doesn't matter what triggered the argument; we were just really bad at fighting. A small issue escalated into global status in Nano seconds. Did we *really* have that much shit between us? Would we ever be capable of accepting each other, or were we doomed to "win" arguments by proving who was right and who was wrong? Did we have realistic expectations for our marriage?

Like most couples, we usually had variations of the same three or four arguments. I thought the problem was his inability, or unwillingness, to be empathetic. Maybe the real problem was my expectation that he would change, simply because I want him to be different. What would happen if I just listened to him, even though I knew what he was going to say before he did? I had to let go. I also had to stop over-explaining myself, become a better listener, use fewer words to get my point across, and stop interrupting—something that only made things worse.

To be honest, his complaints against me were not new. I'd heard the same things in past relationships. Either I was choosing the same man repeatedly, or there were things about me I would have to change if I wanted this marriage to last. Having great verbal skills does not give someone the right to cross-examine their spouse. More than one man has told me that I would make a great prosecuting attorney. In fact, a marriage counselor once told my soon-to-be-ex-husband that he shouldn't even try to win an argument with me because he was out-gunned. At the time, I took pride in that endorsement. Now, I see it differently.

I'd been blaming Howard for my misery, but **I** was the one who signed on to this trip; **I** chose retirement; **I** got rid of my belongings; and **I** remained silent, when I should have spoken up. **I** was the one who chose compliance over authenticity.

I was the architect of the majority of the pain in my life.

As we passed miles and miles of Texas Bluebonnets, my monkey-mind interrupted long enough to whisper about having no place to go if this trip derailed completely. I didn't have a home anymore, it hissed, and neither of my siblings was in a position to help. The few things I had left were stacked in a 10' x 30' storage unit back in the desert, along with my car, whose battery was probably dead by now. How much would I have to save before I had enough for a decent place to live? How hard would it be to find a dog-friendly place to live? My mind raced on and on until the circle was complete, with me in the center as a homeless person destined to die alone, probably in the rain. This train of thought had a well-grooved track and took less than five seconds to run its course.

The potholes got worse. Three in a row introduced a sharp pain down the back of my left leg, followed by hot twinges in my neck. We were an hour outside of Austin. I had no idea how we would fake our way through the visit with his daughter.

I kicked my monkey-mind to the curb and refocused: we were going to make it. No one was leaving; we were just having a bad day.

CHAPTER 28

HOMELAND SECURITY AND GIANT MOSQUITOES

We had a fun three days with Danielle and Brett. Howard and I put on our game faces and faked it so well that we actually pulled out of our nosedive and had a great time at their house. In addition to visiting with Danielle and Brett, we had dinner with a former work colleague, his wife, and their two young daughters. The kids were still young enough to think their parents hung the moon; we loved being around them. I was grateful for our short time in Austin, and ready for our next stop: Houston.

It may only take five minutes for the International Space Station to travel from California to Houston, but it took us the better part of the afternoon to get there from Austin. We found an RV Park near the Houston Space Center and, although it was next to the freeway, we quickly paid for a spot for the night. The next day, we got to the Space Center early. We parked in the over-size parking lot, filled Emmy's food and water dishes, and hid treats for her to find while we were gone. It was a cool day, so we lowered the shades in the RV, skipped the air conditioner, and turned on the ceiling fan to pull in outside air and keep it circulating through open windows. Howard had taken Emmy for a very long walk earlier that morning, so she was ready for a long nap while we toured the Space Center.

Security was understandably tight. We joined a long queue to the entrance and politely refused the souvenir photo option. They told us that it was not an option. The photos were proof of who had been present that day, should anything bad happen.

That's when I remembered.

We boarded the tram for our one-hour tour when I realized what I'd done and started to sweat. I couldn't make eye contact with the security guards patrolling on foot, because I was sure they could read my mind about hiding something (and they would be right). I had a small baggie of my father's cremains in my back pocket, and it didn't occur to me until that moment, that a baggie of what looked like white powder might be probable cause to be thrown facedown to the sidewalk and handcuffed. Would they believe me that it was just my German rocket-scientist father? It seemed like such a good idea earlier that morning; I wanted to scatter a small portion of his cremains near the Saturn V rocket exhibit. After all, he helped to develop it.

I decided it would be best not to chance it and kept the baggie sealed; I did not have what it took for a life of crime.

We looked at exhibits for the rest of the morning, including moon rocks and an array of space suits behind glass. I got goose bumps looking at Sally Ride's space suit. She was the first American woman to go into space in 1983, and it reminded me of how insignificant I felt after reading about her historic flight. She was a year older than I was, and had accomplished so much; I was the mom of a 2-year old in 1983, deeply depressed, and in a dysfunctional marriage with an alcoholic.

It didn't take long for Howard's feet to get itchy again. He wanted to see Galveston before the end of the day, so we quickly marched through the rest of the exhibits, Clark-Griswold-style, before splitting a sandwich in the RV on our way to Galveston. It took a little over three hours.

The only thing I knew about Galveston was that Glen Campbell sang a song about it (something about cleaning his gun and thinking about Galveston) and that they had had two big hurricanes. The first was at the turn of the 20th century, where over 6,000 people had died; the second—Hurricane Ike—occurred in the early morning hours of September 13, 2008. Hurricane Ike hit Galveston with 110 mph winds and a 22' storm surge, destroying boats, smashing houses, flooding thousands of homes, uprooting trees, and cutting electric power to millions of customers. The town of Galveston has never been the same, according to a resident we met in a very cool little Galveston neighborhood called Cedar Lawn. Cool, because most of Galveston was on a grid, and Cedar Lawn rebelled against the grid and put in winding streets instead, for a more colorful personality. Our new friend saw us cruising through the neighborhood in Sonward (we were hard to miss) while she was clipping the shrubs in her front yard. She called out to see if we would be interested in buying her house! We talked for at least a half an hour as she pointed to empty houses on the street and told stories about her former neighbors who had fled after Hurricane Ike, and have never been back. She offered to give us a tour of her beautiful two-story home on a corner lot, but we politely declined, saying that we were not ready to buy just yet. With a slap on the hood, she thanked us for talking to her and got back to her bushes.

Next, we headed towards the gulf and passed scores of pastel Easter-egg colored houses on stilts overlooking the water, reminding me that Easter was just a few days away. Just for fun, we pulled a few brochures out of Plexiglas boxes on the homes for sale, and were stunned to realize how affordable my dream house on the beach would be in Galveston—if only we were willing to live in a hurricane-zone.

After lunch at Gaidos, a famous seafood spot across the street from the water, we decided to go back to Houston to see if we could make the Astros Game that night. It was a nice day, so we decided to take Emmy for a walk on the beach— big mistake.

I was looking at the water in the gulf, wondering why it was brown, when Emmy began rolling in a huge pile of dried seaweed. Suddenly, she jumped up and began shaking her head violently. I called out to her, but she couldn't open her eyes because a huge swarm of sand fleas was orbiting her head. I grabbed her by the collar and pulled her into the surf, thinking water would get rid of the fleas—wrong again! Now she had fleas attacking her eyes and ears, as well as mosquitoes the size of humming birds going after the rest of her body. I tried smacking them to death until I realized I was also smacking my poor dog.

All the way to Houston, Emmy kept looking at me with eyes that said, "What the hell?"

CHAPTER 29

BASEBALL, GOLF, AND EASTER SUNDAY

We made it back to Houston in time to see a great baseball game at Minute Maid Park. The Astros were playing Colorado, and Howard scored great seats from what he likes to call "an unnamed individual outside the gate." Highlights included seeing George and Barbara Bush rooting for their home team, cold beer, and sizzling hot dogs with spicy mustard. Life was good for us, but not so much for Emmy.

We got back to the RV after the game and it was obvious that she had been licking her mosquito bites and scratching her ears non-stop. Fortunately, the RV Park had a dog wash station, so we gave her a thorough rinsing the next morning, hoping to rid the last of the salt water from her thick fur and provide some relief from the itching.

We were on our way to Little Rock, Arkansas, when the skin on Emmy's belly and back legs turned bright red beneath her fur. She licked and scratched until there were open sores; we knew she needed more help than we could give her, and started looking for a place to stop. After calling every local Veterinarian we could find on Easter Sunday, only to get recordings, there was nothing to do but wait another day. In the meantime, I clipped the fur on her legs and belly to help dry the matted areas caused by her licking. Then I gave her Benadryl for the itching (after checking the Internet for the correct dosage, based on her weight) and offered her a treat. She declined.

Finally, after spending Easter Sunday watching six hours of the Masters Golf Tournament (one of us watched, one of us sulked—you do the math) in a hotel room in a *dry* county in Arkansas, we found a great Veterinarian in Little Rock on Monday morning. He gave Emmy a steroid shot, antibiotics, spray-on cooling gel, and some nasty smelling heartworm medicine. She immediately felt a lot better and took a long nap in the air-conditioned RV while Howard and I visited the Bill Clinton Library (very, very, interesting and did not at all resemble a doublewide trailer, as we were warned). Afterwards, we took the long way to check out Hot Springs, Arkansas, before heading to Catherine's Landing, an RV resort with bragging rights to a wine bar. The stop after Hot Springs would be Little Rock, for a visit with our friends, Cynthia and Jerry.

As we were driving through Hot Springs, I noticed a blue and white Hofbrauhaus logo on the side of a building. The Hofbrauhaus is a famous brewery and pub in Munich, Germany, and the origin of Oktoberfest. Years earlier, Howard and I spent the better part of an afternoon in the Hofbrauhaus in Germany, but it was my childhood memories that came flooding back the second I saw the logo. Although I was only four years old, I have sharp memories of my parents taking us to Oktoberfest there. My parents even took a picture of me posing in a sad little party hat with my arm wrapped around a huge beer stein. Now, we were looking for an authentic German restaurant in the middle of Arkansas.

It felt like hours before we found a parking place, because Howard will rarely take the first available spot. In my never-to-be-humble opinion, he will pass completely good parking spots in search of the *perfect* parking spot. Tempers were running high when the *perfect* spot finally opened up. I leaped out of the RV while the engine was still running in anticipation of great German food. I didn't even mind the long walk to the restaurant. You can imagine how my little heart fell, after seeing the sign on the door. It was Monday—the only day of the week that they were closed.

After more walking around, we finally settled on a small Italian place with Clos du Bois on the wine list and enjoyed a somewhat leisurely dinner before driving through the dark to Catherine's Landing for the night.

The next day was devoted to exploring Hot Springs, Arkansas, whose motto is "America's First Resort". We toured the old bathhouses and admired the walk-of-fame tributes to hometown heroes such as Bill Clinton and Billy Bob Thornton. We filled our water bottles with hot water, straight out of the fountain in the middle of town, which supposedly had healing properties. Emmy drank an entire bowl and seemed to improve. It was a great town with just the right number of touristy shops and wide sidewalks—the kind of town where you just knew everyone went to the Friday night high school football game. There were things to see and nice people to meet.

Speaking of nice people, Hot Springs is like many cities in the south. Everyone stops to say hello. They want to find out a little more about you, like where your people came from, and how you like their town. All that small town charm can be endearing or it can be downright annoying, if all you want is directions to the interstate without first climbing your family tree.

A woman pulled up beside us at a red light, rolled down her window and barked, "Where y'all from?" Howard answered vaguely, "Oh, everywhere." When she pointed out that we had California plates, he said, "Yeah, well—we've been through there, too," which struck me as odd. I would wear the California state flag as a t-shirt if I could. I am not the least bit hesitant about being from California, especially in the south, where they supposedly do not care for the "left" coast. She looked at him as if he were running from the law and beat us off the line when the light turned green.

"Why didn't you tell her we were from California?" I asked. (Howard said later that it was more of a demand.)

"Why do you have to criticize everything I say or do?" he answered.

Two people, both with their panties in a bunch, made their way next to Little Rock, Arkansas, for a visit with Cynthia and Jerry.

CHAPTER 30

MELTDOWN

Cynthia and I worked together at the same publishing company. She was one of a group of sassy GRITS (**G**irls **R**aised **I**n **T**he **S**outh), and I loved her. Still do. Cynthia didn't suffer fools gladly, which accounted for her track record of either making life-long friends or enemies of people very quickly. Although Cynthia and I didn't work together directly—I was in sales management and she was in professional development—we found ways of connecting when possible.

For example, I got a call from her the year before I retired asking if I still had a sales rep in San Francisco. When I told her I did, she asked me if I was overdue for a ride-along with said sales rep—hint-hint. It turned out that Cynthia was going to be in San Francisco on business and wanted me to meet her there for a little retail therapy, "if I could swing it." I could, I did, and it was a blast. That was also the last time I had seen Cynthia. When she found out I had retired and that we would be traveling throughout the country, she insisted that we stop by for a visit with her and her own Mr. Wonderful, Jerry.

Early on, Cynthia was one of the few people in whom I had confided my doubts about my relationship with Howard. During the first year Howard and I lived together at my place in Thousand Oaks, there were many days spent in saturated silence. The more I tried to get Howard to talk about what was bothering him, the more he would shut down. Cynthia called to say hello one morning and I just couldn't fake a cheerful demeanor. When she asked me what was wrong, I broke down in tears. She listened as I rambled on and didn't offer advice until I asked.

"Honey," she said. "Have a good, long, cry before you dry those tears. Then pack his bags and do not look back. He doesn't love you the way you want to be loved."

Years later, when I told her we were getting married, she was the first to send me an engagement gift—note cards engraved with my future name, *Sonja Millings,* on the front. We never talked about that morning again.

I was a little nervous about how comfortable our visit would be, but I didn't need to worry. They greeted us at the front door with big smiles and a doggie bowl of water for Emmy. They had a beautiful house in a neighborhood with rolling hills, lush landscaping, and homes right out of *Architectural Digest.* Their back yard had a deck and shade trees for Emmy. Everything about their home was welcoming and immediately put us at ease. Howard supervised, while Jerry fired up the barbeque, both cradling bottles of beer. Cynthia and I sat on the deck with our wine and gossiped about former bosses. We were originally only going to spend one night, but once Jerry started bragging about his favorite golf course, Howard changed his mind. Apparently, I was not the only one who missed civilization.

The next few days in Little Rock went by fast; clothes shopping with Cynthia, drinking vodka Martinis with Jerry while watching Judge Judy every afternoon at 4:00, the boys with their golf, and more shopping. One afternoon, Cynthia took me on a tour of the surrounding neighborhoods to see quaint cottages, custom homes with landscaped yards, specialty shops within walking distance, and all the amenities you would need to be happy and healthy.

I got quiet. When she asked me what was wrong, I told her how difficult it had been to spend 24 hours a day together and how much I missed having a home. Instead of a lecture, she looked at me and said, "I could never do what you're doing. I have to have my things around me; I have to know where I'm going to sleep at night—preferably in my own bed; I have to *feel* my house around me; I have to get away from Jerry on a regular basis. I've spent too much time becoming this woman (she gestured from head to foot), to turn my back on her now."

I didn't know whether to feel relief or despair. She acknowledged that I was not being selfish to feel so hopeless about the success of the trip. In ten seconds, she understood why I was struggling. I'd spent hours trying to explain this to my husband and feeling like a jerk when I saw the disappointment in his eyes. I was not crazy—I had been in over my head from the beginning. I was beginning to face the realization that Howard and I might have very different values.

Cynthia's compassion released a flood of grief about all kinds of loss, the most recent being my house. I no longer had my house in Thousand Oaks. I sold it at a terrible loss because, although the rent covered the mortgage, it did not cover the property taxes; insurance; HOA fees; water; trash; the cost of maintenance; the property managers; or the constant repairs and maintenance on a townhouse that was 35 years old. What little equity I had after four years was lost in the housing crash. Once I no longer drew a paycheck, I couldn't keep shelling out over $1,000 a month to carry a house worth 44% of what I paid for it. Because the original profit I made when I sold my house in Sacramento went into the down payment for my townhouse in Thousand Oaks, I had no equity to leverage for my next house.

Nor did I have my things. I sold everything piece-meal at a variety of garage sales and on Craigslist.

Lastly, I no longer had my career, a great paycheck, or feedback about my performance (those damn gold stars again).

I had voluntarily given away my independence and a huge chunk of my identity. No wonder I was depressed, pissed off, and tired of trying to put on a happy face every day.

CHAPTER 31

HOME AND HEART

It was a quiet ride to our next stop: Kansas City, Missouri. Cynthia made a lot of sense. I couldn't imagine her going along with Jerry if she didn't want to do something. It wouldn't do for Cynthia to say *no*. She would say *Hell, no!*

Before we left, she told me that the only place Jerry was the undisputed leader in their marriage was on their boat; a boat can have only one Captain. She completely trusted him in an emergency and gladly took orders under those circumstances; however, back on dry land it was a different story. Jerry was a smart man. He and Cynthia had been married long enough for him to know that it was best if Cynthia had the last word 99% of the time, especially when it came to things of the heart or home.

There it was again—heart and home—the two elusive things that kept me up at night. Of course, it helped that Jerry was a pretty roll-with-it kind of guy who dearly loved his wife and put her happiness above his most of the time. He had confidence in her decisions and gladly stepped aside when it came to home projects, like decorating the guest room or hiring a painter. She backed off when it came to things like buying a new barbeque, because he had dominion over all things outdoors. Their long-term marriage was a dance that worked.

Epiphany: Except that marriage is not a boat. It is more like a race with random obstacles, distractions, and different styles of running. I am a sprinter and Howard is a marathon runner (thank God). Marriage requires a series of negotiations. The best you can hope for is to manage problems and give up the idea that everything can be fixed. I was good at negotiation and management in my professional life—maybe I should have used those skills in my marriage, instead of running so purely on emotion.

During the long ride to Kansas City, my thoughts once again drifted towards what seemed like a lifelong search for a home. We moved around a lot when I was a kid, but my mother made a beautiful home wherever we went. She would unpack our bedrooms first—complete with fresh sheets on the bed—to help us adjust to our first night in the latest new house. She arranged small things on the windowsill above the sink in the kitchen— ceramic birds, tiny stone cottages, and always a planter or two filled with succulents. I would concentrate on these items as I dried the dishes and made up stories in my head about the birds or the stone cottages. To this day, I love to wash and dry dishes by hand. I still let my imagination run wild as I put the last of the pans away.

Colorful area rugs not only preserved the wall-to-wall carpeting, but also added splashes of color in the family room, with matching runners in the hallway. My father's paintings from Germany would hang in the same rooms of different houses; the oil painting of the peaceful valley in Bavaria always hung over the TV; an abstract of wolves on a cliff overlooking a river hung near the desk in his office. The two colored-pencil drawings of the marketplace in Sondershausen, Germany, would flank the hutch in the dining room.

My parents planted trees, rose bushes, flowers, shrubs, and vegetables. They found room for potted plants on the patio, wind chimes in the trees, and a small fountain near the back fence. They would transform an ordinary tract house in an average neighborhood into a stunning botanical retreat. Making and keeping your house and yard in order was just part of being German (or so I was told), regardless of property boundaries. I still remember how the neighbors would peek from behind their curtains as my mother swept the sidewalk in front of our house every morning, even though it was technically the city's property.

Maybe it's in my DNA. I may have inherited my yearnings for a home from my mother. I can't believe she was only 34 years old with three children, when my dad (already in his 50s) told her they were moving to America. I can only imagine what it would have been like for her to leave her family and everything she knew, with a man who had a hard time showing tenderness and compassion—not to mention the challenge of having to learn a new language! In spite of her outward sense of humor, playfulness, and nurturing style of parenting, she suffered from migraines and battled depression throughout most of my life.

As the miles dragged on, I started a mental list of all the places I had lived. I was not surprised that, when I was a kid, I went to six schools in twelve years, and had moved 26 times up to that point in my life. Where was #27 going to be?

After a quick stop at Subway for lunch, we were back on the road, but I was not quite ready to let go of my review of all the houses in which I had lived. Did I feel at home in all of them, any of them, or somewhere in between? I tried to remember the last place in which I'd felt at home and at peace: it was Thousand Oaks.

Ironically, there was never a doubt that the city of Thousand Oaks was my true home, but the townhouse—not so much. There were moments when I felt pride of ownership, but mostly I cursed the stairs and resented the expense. It was a beautiful townhouse spanning three floors and almost 2,200 square feet; much more house than I needed, but the housing market was limited, and I felt pressure to make a decision. My new company was getting tired of paying for temporary housing. Again—I was not thinking strategically. I bought the townhouse out of desperation and spent way over my budget, taking small comfort in its eventual resale value (HA!), unlike my Sacramento house. I had always planned to pay off my mortgage on the Sacramento house. I planted trees, updated the bathrooms, laid hardwood flooring, installed a small waterfall in the back yard, and spent many a rainy night in the spa, wearing only my Sacramento River Cats baseball hat. One of my favorite rituals was an evening glass of wine while sitting in my backyard and listening to the wind as it made its way through the canopy of trees surrounding my property. I loved my house in Sacramento, and yet, once I made the decision to accept the job in Thousand Oaks, I couldn't wait to leave. My dream house in Sacramento became just another commodity that I would have to liquidate for my new life in Thousand Oaks. A seemingly random series of events, including my daughter transferring to Long Beach State University in Southern California; dangerous stress levels from a high-pressure job; a lawsuit against the handyman company I'd hired for sending a felon to work on my house (who also robbed me); made the decision easier. I was ready for a new start in a beautiful city near the water. In the back of my mind, I wondered how long I could be happy there before needing a new distraction.

My happiness expiration date seemed to be around the two-year mark for both work and relationships. After two years, I would usually get restless or bored and begin to look for something new to learn or someone new to love.

When I thought back to the times I'd been the happiest, it had always been when I was doing what I loved, rather than losing myself in a relationship. I had no trouble being alone for months—or even years—and loved the freedom and integrity of that life. Eventually I would miss the intimacy and companionship of a relationship. I still wanted to be a part of a family that loved and took care of each other. I was a serial monogamist, with most relationships lasting around 4 years. In truth, they died of natural causes at the end of year two, but it would take another two years to extricate myself, usually in the form of a huge blow-up with no hope of returning to the scene of the crime.

As we blew down the highway with the lights of Kansas City in sight, I had another epiphany. With the exception of the year I was pregnant with my daughter, the happiest times in my life had been *between relationships* when I'd been under the influence of my own thoughts, without having to compromise myself in order to keep peace.

Home and heart—intricately connected and filled with longing, searching for permanence and fearing a short life cycle; interchangeable. I could not keep living for something outside of myself, nor could I keep letting fear be the tiebreaker for major life decisions. Lastly, I could not keep delaying happiness until I fixed the broken parts of me.

CHAPTER 32

KANSAS CITY TORNADO WATCH

I was on emotional overload and looking forward to getting out of my head for a while. I needed to avoid the time machine that kicked in whenever the road stretched out infinitely, giving me too much time to roam through my memories. I'd been to Kansas City several times, always on business, and came home with stories about the friendly people, great restaurants, and abundance of public art. I couldn't wait to show Howard the city!

Our first stop was Kaufman Stadium, for a Royals baseball game against the Cleveland Indians. The home team lost—probably because it was Friday the 13th. The stadium was raucous, but nothing compared to the tailgate parties in the huge parking lot. We left the air conditioner on in the RV for Emmy, who went to sleep almost immediately after a long walk. I remember we were holding hands as we walked through the parking lot, when a drunk guy who was with a bunch of his buddies yelled, "Man, I wish somebody loved me like that!" Both the comment and the courtesy caught me off guard. I guarantee that we would have heard something entirely different in the parking lot of Dodger Stadium in Los Angeles. I took it as a good omen.

The next day we had one of our longest sightseeing days to date. It began with two museums: the American Jazz Museum, and the Negro League Baseball Museum. Howard liked to linger, and I couldn't wait to see what was next, so we split up to enjoy the exhibits at our own pace. One of these museums alone would have occupied the better part of an afternoon, but both together made for an inspiring day. Their location on 18th and Vine invited us to explore the rest of the neighborhood afterwards. I took a picture of Howard on the corner of "12th Street and Vine" (part of the lyrics to *Kansas City,* written by Lieber and Stoller).

Kansas City is also home to one of my favorite sales reps from my old life in publishing. Steve is a soft-spoken, hard-working, honest, smart, and friendly guy, who regards his customers as friends and vice versa. I'd spent time with him in the field on ride-alongs, and went to bat for him when upper-management wanted to change his successful territory. He was a stellar sales rep and a genuinely nice guy. After a few emails back and forth, Steve, and his wife Linda, invited us to brunch the next morning. First, we had a few more stops before we settled down for what would be a very adventurous night.

I took Howard to see the Nelson-Atkins Museum of Art, smackdab in the middle of the city. My favorite part was the massive lawn with giant shuttlecocks (stop smiling and Google it). We spent hours roaming throughout the grounds, admiring the sculptures and statues—some tucked into hiding places—as well as their giant friends on the lawn. We didn't even make it inside the museum before running out of time. We had to beat the crowds at Arthur Bryant's, reputed to be the best barbeque joint in the world.

The first thing we noticed about Arthur Bryant's was the ordinary neighborhood and humble building. After we parked and walked for a block or so, the smell of barbeque smoke hit us, and we stepped up our pace. They had no dress code, great prices, and many yummy options on the menu board. It was on the early side for dinner, yet there was still a long line to the counter. We entertained ourselves by looking at the pictures of celebrities that lined the walls. You could tell who was a local, because they rattled off their order without hesitation, while the rest of us stared at the myriad of options on the big wooden menu above the counter. Howard and I usually split one dinner, but not in this case; he got the pulled pork sandwich and I got a small rack of the baby backs (my mouth is watering as I write this). We were fortunate to have gone early but still had to compete for a table, and by the time we'd finished eating, the line went around the block.

Afterwards, we waddled around a very trendy downtown area in an attempt to digest. Beer helped. It was an almost-perfect day, but Emmy was waiting patiently back in the RV and we were ready for an early night.

Fat chance.

We checked into an RV Park on the edge of town near the Worlds of Fun amusement park, which, fortunately, was still closed for the season. The nice woman who checked us in asked polite questions ("where y'all from?") before letting us know that the tornado might miss us tonight, or might not.

Wait—what?

"Just listen for the siren and head for the brick restrooms if they go off—it's okay to bring the dog along with you", she said with a drawl.

We just stared at her. We'd been so focused on our whirlwind afternoon and evening, that we completely missed the storm warnings throughout the day. I dropped my happy-tourist face and asked her how she could be so casual about a tornado.

"Happens every year about this time—don't forget, we have free coffee in the morning."

She was actually chirpy; I could not believe my ears. Who lives like that? She must have read my mind, because she glanced at our registration card and mumbled something about earthquakes in California, and how she would rather take her chances with a "lil' bit of wind" in God's country instead of worrying about the earth moving. Then she turned away and wished us a good night over her shoulder.

We parked in a spot with a great view of the roller coaster next door and discussed what to do for the rest of the night. Sleep was out of the question. Instead, we turned on the TV and watched the news as the wind began to rock Sonward. Steve sent a text, inviting us to ride out the storm with him and Linda, but we were already settled for the night and had a plan in case things got bad (brick restrooms). Besides, we didn't want to be the city-slickers who freaked out about "a lil' bit of wind". The news station we were watching was in Wichita, Kansas. At one point, they announced that the tornado was heading toward their studio, and that they would have to suspend their broadcast and evacuate the staff to a nearby storm shelter. They were only 200 miles away!

The metallic taste of the air instantly took me back to Huntsville, Alabama, in the mid-1960s, when my family and I stayed up all night during our first tornado. My mom stacked our coats near the front door, in case we had to leave suddenly. No one really thought about how useless a coat would be if a tornado leveled our house, but it didn't matter as long as we had a plan.

I didn't get worried until Emmy started pacing and softly whimpering. She was agitated, restless, and had huge eyes. I tried to comfort her, but she was highly distracted by something outside the door. I was so preoccupied with Emmy that I didn't notice when the RV began to rock, first gently, and then more forcefully. We could hear the glassware in the cupboards clinking together. I worried briefly about lightening hitting the satellite dish on the roof. There was lots of thunder, but no rain. We had already converted the couches into our bed, so the three of us got under the covers, turned out the lights, and rode out the storm. I finally fell asleep with the Wicked Witch of the West's instrumental theme song from the Wizard of Oz playing through my mind.

We were lucky, but not Wichita. They suffered hundreds of millions of dollars in damage. Fortunately, no lives were lost.

We awoke to a beautiful sunny day with more than enough time for brunch with Steve and Linda, who were equally casual about the tornado. I reminded Steve about the time we were on a conference call together. His heavy breathing made it sound like he was pacing. When I asked him about it, he calmly replied that he was going to the basement because the siren was indicating a tornado in the vicinity. He actually had to calm me down, 1,500 miles away in California! I asked about Linda and he said that she was at work but he wasn't worried. They had a good building with storm walls.

People who live in the path of tornados are made of strong stock—salt of the earth. I could never get used to it, let alone rebuild, and carry on.

We finished our brunch and gave Steve and Linda a quick tour of Sonward before hitting the Harry S. Truman Library on our way out of town. After hugs good-bye, I could have sworn I heard them talking about how hard it must be to take a yearlong road trip in such a small RV, and how they would never be able to spend all that time alone. I guess we're salt of the earth, too. Or crazy.

CHAPTER 33

A WORD ABOUT DOGS

When it comes to traveling with a dog, the #1 rule is that their needs come first. That's good advice at home, too.

Do *not* get a dog spontaneously. Walk away from the stranger with a boxful of puppies at the farmers market, if you even slightly suspect it will end up alone in the back yard after the newness wears off. Do not complain when your dog jumps on people, pees in the house, and "behaves badly," as though neglect and lack of training were somehow the dog's fault. If you can't fully accept a dog as part of your family, don't get a dog. A pet is not a fashion accessory, nor is it a toy for young children who will soon grow bored with it. Most children will not feed nor walk a dog as promised, and will definitely not learn responsibility from the experience. Instead, they will learn how to manipulate their parents for short-term rewards. They might also learn that moms usually end up doing the dirty work.

Dogs are pack animals, and to isolate them in the back yard is torture—they *need* to be a part of the family.

I got Molly and Emily (Emmy) in 2000, because I needed a dog in my life to offset my daughter's eventual flight out of the nest. Her absence would leave a huge hole in my life. I did a ton of research into traits of various breeds and decided that Golden Retrievers were the best fit for my situation. Lyndsay saw Emily and fell in love with her feistiness and that wonderful puppy-breath. Then I saw Molly, Emily's littermate, and I knew we had to get them both.

Because they were my first dogs, I had no idea how to train them but I knew enough to know I needed help. Many places offered classes in dog obedience. Before deciding which one to sign-up for, I observed several classes and immediately rejected the ones who used harsh methods and choke chains. I finally found a wonderful trainer, who believed in asserting dominance, but used humane methods and reinforced good behavior with positive rewards.

In other words, I took my role as their human very seriously.

I took the puppies everywhere with me, so they spent a lot of time around little kids, other dogs, cats, and crowds. I poured affection on them at every opportunity, but also made sure they knew I was the alpha-dog of the house. The pack runs better when everyone knows who is in charge. My daughter used to smile and call me the head bitch.

More than once, the evening ended early because my date didn't like dogs, or used harsh words when they nosed his hand for a pat on the head. I knew I could never be in a relationship with a man who didn't like my dogs. When Howard and I got together, not only did I fall in love with him, but the dogs did, too. He was always the first one out the door to the dog park, and would throw the Frisbee non-stop until Molly was panting so hard that I made them both stop for a water break. He didn't tease me when I had to travel for work and got an overnight dog sitter, nor did he roll his eyes when I steamed broccoli for them as a special treat. He grew to love them as much as I did. He was with me when we took Molly to the beach one last time before going to the animal hospital when it was time to have her euthanized to end her suffering (and begin ours).

We were a tight little pack before, but traveling with Emmy took us to another level of love and companionship. Howard's first thought upon waking each morning was to take Emmy for a walk—it was also the last thing he did at night. We made sure to pull over every few hours so that she could stretch her legs. Her water bowl was always full and she had a soft pad to sleep on in case the floor got chilly. She also had a blanket on the couch in the RV on which to sleep while we were driving. The few times that she got carsick, I held a plastic bag under her chin so she could throw-up at 60 mph. I can honestly say that there was never a time that we got mad at her, or wished she had stayed home.

When it came time to find a pet-friendly hotel, we were happy to pay the $10-$25 pet fee. At the time, La Quinta Inn was our favorite because they were clean, didn't charge for pets, and sometimes even had treats for Emmy upon check-in. There were other times when hotels charged a non-refundable pet fee of $100-150. At those times, we just kept driving.

In all honesty, there were a few times when fatigue and lack of options created a new super-hero: Clandestine Dog. Able to sneak into a hotel as though she owned the place! Never once barking, peeing, pooping, or otherwise disturbing the footprint of the hotel room! Sleeping on her RV blanket, so as not to leave so much as a hair behind!

That was the situation as we crossed the Missouri River and decided to spend the night at a very high-end casino, whose front desk clerk confirmed over the phone that they were dog-friendly but was unsure of the pet fee. She guessed around $30—tops. She transferred us to two other people in an effort to confirm the fee, but no one really knew. Hours later, when Howard approached the front desk to check us in, they said that the non-refundable pet fee was $150 for dogs under 15 pounds. Larger dogs were not allowed (Emmy hovered closer to 64 lbs.). It is a good thing that Emmy and I stayed in the RV while Howard was at the front desk, because we ended up taking a room and smuggled Clandestine Dog past the front desk.

Looking back, I realize how risky this was. Some hotels charge the room rate plus up to $250 if they catch you sneaking a pet in. We didn't even think about people with pet dander allergies! It's a poor excuse, but we were tired, pissed-off at the hotel for their lack of knowledge about their own pet policy, and neither of us could face another night in the RV so soon after our brush with death in Kansas City.

However, if you do decide to break the law and sneak your dog into a dog-friendly, but insane-pet-fee hotel, we found that using a side exit as an entry point works well, in spite of the security cameras.

CHAPTER 34

WHINE AND JEEZ

Two years before we set off on our trip, I read about a little town in Missouri called Hermann. I was researching German communities in America after waking up from a dream in which our next home was located in a city with a rich German history. We were living in the desert community at the time, and I'm sure that my subconscious was searching for a lifeline to get me through the hot, dry summer.

Coincidentally, their website described Hermann as a "dream city," established in 1837 as a German Society settlement.

Hermann is nestled along the banks of the Missouri River and looks like a beautiful German town. I studied their website and read all about the original architecture, prize-winning wineries, and variety of specialty shops. I *had* to see it for myself.

I signed-up on their email list that night. Checking the calendar of events, I learned that national bike race routes wound through town, there were seasonal events on the wine trail, annual blues festivals—you name it, they had it all. I couldn't believe it—all that beauty, plus wine and a German heritage? I hounded Howard for a long weekend in Hermann, and he always had the same response: "Let's wait until after we retire so we can visit for a long time, not just a weekend."

Finally—we were on our way to Hermann!

One of our first stops was the Stone Hill Winery, where we learned that the original Germans had purchased land in Hermann sight-unseen. Once they got there and realized how difficult farming would be, they planted vineyards on the side of hills instead of crops on the flat land they were expecting. We decided to eat lunch before taking a tour of the Stone Hill Winery, and quickly found the best German food in town at the Vintage Restaurant, a former carriage house and horse barn, right there on the winery grounds. According to the menu, it was nominated as the "Best German Restaurant in America" by GermanDeli.com. I had the German pork roast with mashed potatoes and gravy, red cabbage, and lots of bread with thick butter. Howard ordered the Schnitzel plate. He had lemonade and I ordered the Stone Hill Chardonnay, which came in a heavy glass goblet as big as a water glass—bliss. The meals were huge, so I ended up ordering a second glass of wine.

I'm sure it's obvious by now that my husband and I sometimes have different definitions of a good time. His were more about being out in nature and walking, walking, walking, through all kinds of interesting environments, and mine were about stopping to smell the roses and sample the wine along the way. By now we were getting on each other's nerves more each day over stupid things. I grew to resent the spontaneous side-trips to see yet another natural wonder, and he didn't like the vodka in the freezer, or my second glass of wine at dinner. He wasn't crazy about my first one either, or the fact that wine became my escape. Whenever he watched a ball game in the RV on satellite TV, I downloaded another book on my Kindle and looked for the wine opener. After a while, his disapproval actually fed my rebellious side. We'd had more than one conversation about my drinking and the person I became after "one too many." I argued that his disapproval fueled my attitude, and he countered that I was in denial.

The chasm over alcohol began about six months after we first met, when Howard decided to stop drinking, or at least reduce drinking alcohol to rare or social occasions. One day, he just decided he would be better off without it. I'd heard a lot about his wild younger days and respected him for wanting to live a healthier lifestyle. Even though I admired his ability to make such a big (to me) change, I made it clear that I wouldn't be joining him in his abstinence.

I grew up in a house where the liquor cabinet was as much a natural part of the house as the couch or dining room table. My parents kept wine and beer on hand for guests, but my dad also had a beer with his dinner on most nights (always German beer, of course), and my mom would have a very small glass of wine on special occasions. From a very early age on, if you wanted a sip from their glass, they would give it to you. It was part of the German culture and not a big deal— unlike my friends' parents, who would go to great lengths to lock up their booze, but still got drunk in front of their kids on a regular basis. Getting drunk was definitely not acceptable in our house, but wine or beer with dinner was fine.

Years later, when we were adults and visited my parents, the wine bottle or beer mug was automatically put on the table next to platters of steaming potatoes, succulent pork roast, creamy purple cabbage, tart cucumber salad with oil and vinegar, and lots of thick German bread with butter. My mother was the consummate hostess who never sat down until everyone had everything he or she needed, and then some. God forbid anyone's glass would go dry; ditto for an empty plate. Impossible as it seemed, we always had room left over for apple strudel and coffee or tea. During the winter, my mom added a little brandy to the coffee, or a little rum in the tea "for the lungs." Food was love, and alcohol was merely a hug to go along with it.

Howard was distant throughout our winery tour and ignored me when I asked him what was wrong, even though I knew. I wanted him to say it, so we could come to some kind of compromise, or at least acknowledge his displeasure. When he refused to speak to me, I decided to let him stew while I went to the gift store for a souvenir. I like souvenirs, but Howard, not so much. Screw it, I thought, and bought a refrigerator magnet and t-shirt after browsing for over an hour. We didn't speak for the rest of the night and went through the motions of exploring Hermann the next day. Our visit lasted almost exactly 48 hours—now it was my turn to be resentful. After years of dreaming about Hermann, I felt cheated at how little time we spent there. I didn't trust myself, nor did I want things to escalate any more than they already had, so I said nothing.

On the way to our next stop, St. Louis, my stomach clenched and it felt like I couldn't get air to the bottom of my lungs. I tried to read my Kindle to distract myself, hoping the tension would pass.

Howard woke up the follow morning in St. Louis with baseball on his mind. It didn't take long to find "an unnamed individual" outside the gates at Busch Stadium who had great tickets for sale near the Cardinals' dugout. A few hot dogs and a large beer later— apparently, I had been forgiven—we were cheering for the home team and pretending everything was fine again. The next day, we got caught up on laundry, and I found a salon for a first class haircut and root touch-up, while Howard took Emmy for a long walk.

We spent several days in St. Louis and eventually got back on normal speaking terms. I declined to go to the top of the St. Louis Arch in a small, windowless, pod of death. I believe my exact words were, "Are you fucking kidding me?" To his credit, he admitted that he didn't really want to go up either.

St. Louis is a beautiful city; I'd go back in a heartbeat.

Speaking of hearts, our next stop was one I'd also been looking forward to for years: Graceland, Tennessee—home to heartthrob, Elvis Presley.

CHAPTER 35

SHITTY EX-HUSBAND; WICKED STEPFATHER

It was almost 300 miles from St. Louis, Missouri, to Memphis, Tennessee, and we were still a little distant around each other. It was mostly my fault, because I've always had a hard time moving on without some kind of closure, even if it meant that we "agreed to disagree." An apology would work wonders during these times; it doesn't always have to be about who is right or wrong. Sometimes an apology is just a way to express regret that we were struggling.

There were definitely times when I knew I was being difficult because of fatigue, hunger, or some minor unspoken complaint. During those times, I knew it was best to get a good night's sleep and start fresh the next day. After all, we didn't have to dissect every snide remark. However, when the issues were important and ongoing—like the wine issue, or where we were going to live next, or who controlled the itinerary on our trip—I had a hard time getting past our unresolved arguments. Our communication on that trip needed help, especially when I did my best to ask for what I needed from him and felt like, (a) he didn't hear me or, (b) didn't take me seriously or, (c) thought he knew what I needed better than I did or, (d) all of the above. Upon reflection, my "clear communication" probably sounded a lot like nagging to Howard.

I didn't want to open a can of worms again by having a long drawn-out discussion, which could quickly escalate into another argument, but I needed a way to reconnect. Time and silence were his friends when it came to conflict, but they were my enemies because my mind went into over-drive during those times.

Oftentimes, what you're arguing about is not what you're really arguing about. I could usually tell when my reaction to a trigger was about the situation at hand, or something deeper, something almost primal, having very little to do with him. On the surface, I knew that whatever started the argument didn't warrant a flight response, and yet, to feel safe I had to know where the exits were. I felt the threat in my gut, followed by a sense of free falling and panic. These very real physical symptoms were a red flag that I needed to protect my vulnerability at all costs.

Decades of intermittent counseling couldn't explain the tears that were always close to the surface when it came to trust and intimacy. Theories ranged from being "overly sensitive," to depressed, to low on Vitamin B. Recommendations included regular exercise, and when that didn't work, a wide variety of anti-depressants which made my sex drive go away and wrapped me in an invisible layer of cotton, effectively muffling the world. It kept my depression at bay, but severely changed who I was. The side effects were brutal. Not only did I forget how to poop for a week at a time, but I also lost the ability to tear-up when I saw something that moved me. The upside to being "overly sensitive," was the ability to be emotionally involved with the world. Anti-depressants took that away and turned me into a good girl—compliant, and very, very, dull.

The common thread in counseling was my deep fear in the belief that when it came to being loved, the best I could hope for was temporary and conditional.

It took years of hard work before I stopped trying to fix myself and somewhat accepted my imperfections. This road trip was unraveling my confidence. I would probably always be someone who would "walk with a limp" when it came to intimacy. No amount of therapy, exercise, or Vitamin B, would fix that little kid who was afraid of the dark and couldn't trust the adults to take care of her. However, I found ways of soothing her.

To be truly happy, I had to embrace that limp.

Maybe being "overly sensitive" helped me see things in the world that I might have missed otherwise. Maybe my lack of trust was a valuable survival mechanism in response to an environment that demanded it. Maybe being afraid wasn't the problem—the problem was how often I would let fear stop me.

When it came to defining who I was, I believed the wrong people.

Maybe, just maybe, I was enough.

Epiphany: Every time I ignored my gut, it came back to bite me in the ass.

I got married the first time—barely 18 years old—to escape the chaos and constant bickering between my parents, as well as the mind-numbing boredom of living in a small town with nothing to do. Marriage was my ticket out of Dodge. Next, I married Lyndsay's dad because I believed he would take care of me and wanted a baby as much as I did. He was my ticket to happiness and family bliss. However, there was still another hiccup of a marriage before I finally got it right—decades before I met Mr. Wonderful.

His name was John and he had two young daughters, one in Kindergarten and one in second grade. We'd both been divorced for a few years before we met. It all began when I answered his personal ad (this was before online dating). We got to know each other first over coffee, then later over drinks, and finally made it all the way to dinner. Soon we began to see each other on the weekends when our kids were with the other parent. We waited for months before introducing our kids; we wanted to be sure that they wouldn't get attached prematurely.

Looking back, I realize that we both had unrealistic fantasies and expectations of recreating a "real" family with our little brood, to make up for ripping their tiny hearts out during the divorces. He saw us in the context of *Father Knows Best,* while I leaned more towards *The Brady Bunch.* We had no clue. This was going to be our do-over, a way to patch over the damage caused by our failed marriages.

I was attracted to his devotion to his children, but also cautious about falling for a man whose stories about his past didn't always line up. For example, he made mistakes about the ages of his children by several years in his personal ad, and lied about how old he was at the time of his father's death—things a rational person would never confuse. The inconsistencies were so small at first, that I didn't call him on any of it. Years later, after we were married, I would learn things that I would have expected to surface early on about his family history, like how he and his sister had different fathers. There were hundreds of inconsistencies in the years we were together, for which he always had an explanation or denied outright. I constantly felt off-balance, but just when I was about to break up with him, he would sense it and pull out all the stops to romance me back.

We dated for several years, met each other's families and assumed (as did everyone else) that we would get married someday. There was something huge missing that I couldn't name until years later: trust. I simply could not believe most of what he said. A wise person once told me that if there is a disconnection between words and actions, believe the actions over the words.

It was a come here/go away kind of relationship. If we had long stretches of getting along well and being happy, it meant a big fight was on the horizon. I never knew what would set him off. Once I beat him in tennis and playfully bragged about it over dinner at his mom's house. He pulled me out onto the balcony of her condominium and berated me for humiliating him in front of his family. He told me I would **never** be forgiven and to think seriously about what I'd done—as though he were scolding a 10 year old. Because I had opened up to him too soon, he knew exactly where my vulnerabilities were, and didn't hesitate to hit below the belt when he wanted to make a point. When I called him on it, he always had a good reason for saying what he said. "But it's the truth!" was one of his favorites. It's embarrassing to this day to confess how clueless I was about the signs of a man who was so narcissistic that he refused to make a commitment to me, but strung me along because he didn't want anyone else to have me.

I wish I could have given this little nugget of advice to my younger self:

Never share too soon; never invest more than you are willing to lose; and never, never, believe someone's definition of who you are, unless he or she tells you that you are a goddess.

I was so stunned that I actually believed him; I'd made a huge mistake with my little tennis story, so I apologized, even though my guts were screaming to run as fast and far away as possible. He sat back down at the table and smiled at his girls, continuing to hold court, and laughing freely as though nothing had happened out on that balcony. No one noticed how quiet I'd become.

We finally got to the marriage proposal one night in May after watching his nephew graduate from college in San Francisco. We stopped at a little diner on the way back to Sacramento and he popped the question while we were waiting for our burgers. I should have known—no ring. We talked in the car all the way home and decided to get married in early August, but first he had one little favor: would I give him a day or two to tell his kids? Even though I wanted to wake the kids up as soon as we got home, I reluctantly agreed. He wouldn't tell me why he wanted to wait.

A day or two turned into a month. His newest concern was that his ex-wife would lobby for more money if she knew he was marrying someone with a good career. This made no sense because his ex-wife was married to a professional and not at all concerned with child support. In fact, they had 50-50 custody and money didn't exchange hands outside of expenses related to their children. It was a well-oiled machine. The kids spent every other week at mom's house, alternating weeks at dad's house—schlepping clothes, schoolbooks, and toiletries back and forth.

Speaking of clothes, his kids were not allowed to leave any of "dad's clothes" at mom's house or vice versa. All of their clothing, even underwear and socks, were marked with either an M or a D (Mom or Dad) to indicate from which house the article came. They were just little kids and would invariably leave a "D" shirt at mom's, which was a huge deal for which they could expect a stern talking-to. It hurt me to watch this military precision with the girls in the middle. Eventually, this became a source of conflict between us because I had looser rules about clothes going back and forth for my daughter. I pushed back when he said that we needed to be on the same page when it came to marking underwear with a Sharpie.

However, on the night he proposed, all I could think about was how much I loved his girls, and I looked forward to officially being their step-mom. I was also thrilled that my only child was finally going to have siblings.

We had a barbeque on the Fourth of July, and I still couldn't tell my daughter that I was getting married again. As I put more and more pressure on John to talk to me about what was really going on, he would change the subject and try to distract me with smoke and mirrors. One week before our tentative wedding date, he asked me to meet him for a drink. I was sure he was going to convince me to elope. After ordering our drinks, he took my hands—here it comes, I thought—and said he needed more time.

His ex-wife was acting funny, and he was convinced that she knew about our plans.

I gave the shortest good-bye speech of my life. I simply stood and said, "Fuck you" before walking out without looking back.

For the next three months, John stalked me. He would show up on my doorstep at 7:30 in the morning with coffee and bagels. I refused to answer the door, so he left the food on the front steps. He just happened to be lurking in the produce section of the grocery store on my shopping day. He even wrote a letter of apology to my daughter for the shitty way he treated her and acknowledged that he had issues with her because of the way his stepfather treated him when he was a kid.

I was in counseling at the time, trying to figure out how I had gotten myself into such a cluster-fuck, and asked my therapist for advice. She asked me if I was 100% sure that I was done with him, and if there was even a 1% chance that our relationship might work. After that much time together, of course I had doubts! Then she asked what it would take to consider reconciliation.

The next time I ran into John, I listened to his apologies and asked him if he was serious about getting back together. I saw a glimmer of hope in his eyes. He said he would spend the rest of his life making it up to me if I would give him another chance.

I told him that if he were willing to go to therapy twice a week—once alone, and once as a couple—for a <u>full year</u>, I would consider taking another chance. I was stunned when he agreed and even more stunned when he honored the agreement. A year later, he asked me to marry him again. We were in the kitchen; he was seasoning steaks for the barbeque and I was making cocktails for us. He stopped, took my hands, and asked me if I would marry him. Instead of being thrilled, I deadpanned, "When?" He said, "Two weeks from tonight." I didn't believe him because, although he had given me a timeframe, there was still no ring. I realized he was serious when he said we would tell the kids that night.

Something in my gut turned to stone as soon as we told the girls. I felt as though I had just accepted a job that I was no longer sure I wanted. My requirement for a reconciliation (counseling for a year) was the one thing I never thought he would agree to. I called his bluff and he went all-in. He surprised me and never missed a session in over a year. There was nothing left to do but pick a site, plan a small wedding, and get on with life.

I will skip the marital war crimes that occurred before, during, and after the wedding. It didn't take long until he reverted to being an asshole to my daughter in unspeakably passive-aggressive ways, both large and small. For example, on weekends when all three girls were with us, he would bring home treats for his daughters and say he "forgot" to get one for Lyndsay. It's still too painful to bring up other examples of how emotionally abusive he was to my child. In the beginning, I'd hoped that this was just a normal stepfamily adjustment period, but deep down I knew better.

It wasn't long after the honeymoon that he told me he'd had a change of mind; he wanted me to be his kids' stepmother, but he didn't want to be anyone's stepfather. He felt as though he was "cheating" on his daughters, because my daughter spent more time at the house than they did. I'd been determined to hold this new family together single-handedly if that is what it took, but after he told me his pathetic story, there was nothing left to do. We moved out. Who picks on a child for entertainment?

Shortly after I moved out, an odd thing happened. One Saturday, while I was signing up for a court at our tennis club, the woman behind the desk asked me if I was Sonja _____. I smiled, and said yes, thinking she was being nice by recognizing a regular. However, she didn't have customer service on her mind. She said she was sorry to hear about the pending divorce and wondered if I had figured out what happened. This was a very inappropriate and strange thing for a total stranger to ask. I just stared at her with a confused look on my face. "Maybe he was awful to you because he felt guilty about doing something bad, and drove you away by being mean," she explained.

Who was this woman and what did she know about our marriage? I walked away without comment and later canceled my membership.

At this point, we had been together for over 5 years, although the marriage lasted less than 10 months. You guessed it—I had no sooner moved out when he started coming over again and asking for another chance. It took another year for the divorce to become final because he refused to sign the papers. Even after the divorce was final, he continued to call me on a regular basis or drop by on his way home from the airport after a business trip because "he missed me so much." When I finally told him to leave me alone once and for all, he got married a month later to a woman he had been dating for years.

I chose the wrong man; I didn't listen to my inner wisdom when the red flags started flying; I believed his words instead of trusting my gut; and I believed in his *potential* to be a good husband and step-father, rather than seeing him for who he really was. Worst of all, I thought he was the best I could do. I actually thought I deserved a man who only wanted me when he couldn't have me.

I looked over at Howard with his hands on the steering wheel, singing along with the radio, and truly appreciated what a good man he was. I wanted to be a better wife.

I knew he was the right man, and I knew that I was finally the right woman. I married Howard because I deeply loved him and couldn't imagine my life without him—flaws and all. When I look back at the other marriages, I see agendas based on fear and/or longing. I married Howard full of hope and love.

Still, it didn't change the fact that I was unhappy and felt disconnected. Was it possible to live with integrity, rather than pretend I could continue this road trip for another six months? Could we talk about the hard stuff and come up with a plan that we could both live with?

As we approached the gates of Graceland, I resolved to appreciate my husband and try to overlook the annoying habits that had been driving me crazy, as well as forgive him for things large and small. I was no picnic either. I also committed to being more honest with myself, as well as with my husband, and much gentler—honesty with love. The only time I had been telling the truth lately was during arguments while we were yelling at each other.

My message may have been important, but my delivery was lousy.

CHAPTER 36

MEMPHIS – GRACELAND, SUN RECORDS, COUNTRY MUSIC HALL OF FAME

I'd pictured Graceland to be out in the country somewhere, amidst acres of rolling hills, with sunlight filtering through Magnolia trees. Even though it felt as though we were in the middle of Memphis, we were actually on a 13+-acre estate, nine miles from downtown! We parked in the RV Parking lot and, as we stood in line for tickets, I immediately noticed all the women with big hair wearing commemorative Elvis t-shirts ("The King Lives!"). I expected Tara, the house in *Gone with the Wind*. Instead, it felt more like waiting in line at the haunted mansion at Disneyland. The people-watching alone was worth the price of admission.

We paid $37 per adult and started the group tour in the main mansion, "preserved exactly as Elvis left it." It was kitschy, opulent in a '70s sort of way, and very cool. I was slightly disappointed in the Jungle Room; it looked its age and smelled a bit like mildew. It took about 4 hours to learn everything there was to know about Elvis, his parents, Lisa Marie, and the small army of people necessary to keep everything running. We were getting hungry, but didn't want to stand in a long line for deep-fried peanut butter and banana sandwiches, so we decided to go to Sun Records—home of the Million Dollar Quartet (Elvis Presley, Johnny Cash, Carl Perkins and Jerry Lee Lewis) and a very long list of rockers who got their start with the founder, Sam Phillips. In fact, an unknown Elvis Presley cut his first record there as a gift for his mother. We could have taken a shuttle from Graceland to Sun Records, but decided to drive instead.

The Sun Records tour rocked! We even posed in front of microphone stands used by the rock and roll gods of the 1950s. Other highlights include devouring a Moon Pie in four bites at the diner-inspired snack bar. Howard was in his glory! He was a kid in rock and roll heaven, constantly tugging on my arm to point to a piece of iconic rock history. It made me happy to see him so happy and took no effort on my part to encourage his sense of awe.

We spent the entire next day in Nashville—my new favorite town! It was impossible to keep still; I danced down the sidewalk to whatever music was blasting through the open doors of bars and restaurants along the way. Keith Urban was going to be inducted into the Grand Ol' Opry that evening. As usual, Howard managed to finagle last-minute tickets to this sold-out event; the man has a gift. In the meantime, we decided to go to the Country Music Hall of Fame and Museum. It took an hour of meandering through Nashville before finding a parking spot in a deserted construction site. After making sure Emmy would be okay for a few hours, we set off on foot to learn more about the history of Country music.

I was underdressed.

Regardless of your taste in music, the Country Music Hall of Fame is a must-see. Be prepared to walk. It is huge, with two floors filled to the brim with unique exhibits, each more interesting than the last. People made pilgrimages from all over the world to see things like Hank Williams guitar, which was in the car with him when he died. And the music! You could go into sound booths and hear early original recordings by people I'd never heard of, without whom country music wouldn't have been possible. I liked some old-school country-western music, but tended to lean toward contemporary country music on the radio dial. What an education; I had no idea of the rich history and stories behind the legends. Howard and I held hands and I leaned against him lovingly—we were back to being us again.

CHAPTER 37

HUNTSVILLE, ALABAMA –
U.S. SPACE AND ROCKET
CENTER, AND LYNCHBURG,
TENNESSEE: JACK DANIELS
DISTILLERY TOUR

We were on our way to Huntsville, Alabama!

We began by checking into a hotel on Sunday night (*The Amazing Race* night) in Huntsville, Alabama. The last time I'd been in Huntsville was 1967, when I waved good-bye to that strange world from the back seat of my dad's Mercury Marauder. After living in Huntsville for three long years, my father accepted a position as a rocket scientist at Vandenberg AFB in Lompoc, California. I cannot describe what a relief it was to leave the early 1960s version of the south behind for the Golden State.

As my friend Sherrye would say, "It weren't pretty back in those days." To say there were racial issues would be putting it mildly. Hell, there were even issues against anyone who "talked funny," which meant anyone from the north. George Wallace was the Guvn'r and this Yankee had a rough time at Joe Bradley Junior High. They were still fighting the Civil War in my history class. The south was always within a millimeter of winning some big battle that could have changed the course of the war. Even our textbooks were full of "coulda-woulda-shoulda." I guess it was still pretty fresh. My homeroom teacher had never heard of anyone named Sonja before, so she said I was going to be "Sunny" from now on. The nickname stuck while lived in Huntsville, but I made sure everyone called me Sonja after we moved to California. I should have kept it; it would have been a cool name for a California girl.

Because my values were evolving during those early years in Alabama, I'm grateful for the experience. It solidified my belief in the inherent worth and dignity of every person. In other words, I saw how *not* to be.

Forty-five years later, the people we met in Huntsville couldn't have been more gracious. Southern hospitality was alive and well. After a quick call to my sister for the name of our old street, we were on our way to Kennemore Drive. I found the exact address by Googling *Huntsville/my dad's name/address,* and up popped an old phone book listing which included the street address. In addition to my dad's name, it also included my siblings' names under the phone number: Miss Heidi (yes, they included "Miss") and Pete. My little brother and I were probably too young to be considered, but I wondered why my mother's name wasn't listed. As soon as I read the old phone number, I remembered it.

Back then, we were the first folks in the new Triana Village development. My dad, bless his heart, saw fit to attempt a new world's record for driving from Seattle to Huntsville—over 2,000 miles—and did it in about 3 days. He lost time for potty stops along the way and, man, did we ever hear about it. The policy was to hold it until the car needed gas. My younger brother was lucky, because he got to pee in an old Clorox Bleach jug with the top cut off, which my mother had decorated with our names in rainbow colors. It was bad enough having to watch my brother pee into a jug at 70 mph, but nothing compared to getting hit in the face with urine after my mom rolled down her window to empty the jug from the front seat, without asking me to close my back window.

We even beat the moving truck, which resulted in a couple of nights spent sleeping on the hard floor of our new house. I remember it was a huge house with a giant, pie-shaped back yard. When we moved in, there wasn't one blade of grass, nor tree, shrub, or leaf in site. That would change once my parents unpacked their gardening tools; but for now, there was nothing but red clay. The house looked a little different in 2012: it was teeny-tiny on a corner lot with lots of neighboring homes crowding it. Most of the trees that my dad planted had survived, and were now five times as tall as the roof. I quickly snapped a couple of pictures from across the street, before the current residents came out to see if I was taking surveillance photos for the DEA. We drove by Westlawn Jr. High, where I dearly wanted to attend (Joe Bradley was old, even back then), but other than a few street signs, I had no déjà vu whatsoever. Unlike in Washington, when we drove by my childhood home and I knew every street in the neighborhood, as well as a short cut to Honey Dew Elementary School. Both neighborhoods had deteriorated over time.

It was odd to have harbored so many bad memories about Huntsville, only to realize that it was just another big city. There's a lesson in there somewhere.

I was shaking with excitement about visiting the U.S. Space and Rocket Center in Huntsville. That's where my dad worked in the '60s, although back then it was called Redstone Arsenal. We moved there after Werner von Braun called my father in Seattle and asked him to join the team of German rocket scientists at Redstone—the boys from Peenemunde were together again.

We lucked out, because the main exhibit was a tribute to what would have been Werner von Braun's 100th birthday. They didn't teach a lot about him in school (what with the Civil War and all), so when he and the other Germans from the base occasionally came to the house for dinner, my siblings and I would disappear after introductions. Oh, to go back in time and be a fly on the wall in the living room, with an excellent grasp of the German language! To this day, I wonder what they talked about over coffee and apple strudel.

It was a proud moment to see the Space Center pay tribute to the role of German rocket scientists in the American space race. The tour guide told us that without the Germans, America wouldn't have been able to beat the Russians to the moon. In fact, without the Germans, he mused—who knows how long it would have taken to develop the kind of technology we take for granted today?

This is also the site of Space Camp! We saw small groups of students from late elementary, to middle school-age, dressed in way-cool Space Camp jump suits. They had a whole building dedicated to Space Camp, which was off limits to civilians. According to the brochure, Space Camp lasts from 1-3 weeks, during which time the kids would learn about the space program, run experiments, and go through astronaut training. The gift store employees wore the same cool jump suits—blue with lots of patches of the different missions on the shoulder. I **had** to have one.

This is another must-see. We spent about 4 hours there and could have stayed longer, if not for the Jack Daniels tour in Lynchburg. Yup, we finished-up in Huntsville and hit the road to see our good friend Jack Daniels, but don't tell my other good friend, Johnny Walker.

By the way, I did get a way-cool Space Center jump suit with mission patches. I tried it on over my clothes, right there in the gift shop, and squealed with delight. My husband bought it for me and insisted that I have my name added in gold letters over the left pocket; I will rock on Halloween!

Ron, our tour guide at the Jack Daniels Distillery, would reverently remove his hat every time he uttered the words "Tennessee whiskey." He had all the other men doing it in no time, too! The grounds were carefully landscaped in some places, and wild with local plants in others. The distillery is in the lil' hollow of Lynchburg, Ron explained. He went on to say that Lynchburg is Jack Daniels, and Jack Daniels is Lynchburg—there were no other distractions to get in the way. The entire town is dependent on selling memorabilia and catering to tourists. Even the garbage cans on Main Street are repurposed old JD barrels.

Highlights include seeing the cave where water for *every drop* of Jack Daniels comes from; taking a peek into a 25-foot high vat of JD and breathing deeply with closed eyes; realizing with irony that we were in a dry county; walking the streets of Lynchburg after the tour; finding a Harley Davidson shop that was still open so I could buy a t-shirt for my brother; and of course buying a bottle of Limited Edition Gentleman Jack from the tiny storefront at the distillery, which had a waiver permit to sell alcohol within a special 100 sq. foot room. I may never drink regular Jack Daniels again. Did you know that the Limited Edition is slowly mellowed through ten feet of sugar maple charcoal—twice? It was perfect for sippin' after a long day on the road.

It was dark and cold when we pulled into the RV Park that night, but there was a game on TV (Texas vs. Yankees—Yankees won), the JD was smooth, and I had a new book on my Kindle. Life was good.

Over the next several days, we made our way east to Wilkesboro, North Carolina, to the home of Merlefest, a famous 4-day bluegrass music festival. Merlefest has been an annual event since 1988, and takes place on the beautiful Wilkes Community College campus.

The festival features 13 stages, a no-alcohol policy, delicious and affordable food made and served by civic organizations, very little security (you could easily run into any of the 100+ performers as they made their way from one stage to the next), and a variety of cross-over music. Although the festival features mainly bluegrass, something I had no idea I loved until I heard it, we saw artists from other genres, too. My favorite groups were Steel Wheels, the Steep Canyon Rangers (with Steve Martin on the banjo), the Waybacks, and Wylie Gustafson—who you've heard a million times and didn't know it. He yodels the famous "Yahoooooooooo" for, well, Yahoo. I instantly fell in love with him when I heard his haunting rendition of "Cattle Call" and later bookmarked it on YouTube.

On our way to Merlefest, we hit Dollywood in Sevierville (not at all enticing—didn't even get out of the RV), then Gatlinburg to check out the Great Smokey Mountains National Park. We would have made it further on the Appalachian Trail, had it not been for a lack of bathrooms in the wilderness. Still—we made it a few miles in and back. At one point, I suggested that Howard climb Clingmans Dome without me, and waited patiently in the parking lot with my legs crossed. He got a 360-degree view of the park, and I got another bladder infection.

After four amazing days of music at Merlefest, we pressed on to the transition part of the trip: the point at which I began to feel more comfortable in my skin. Howard enjoys every biome from mountain to desert, and just about every spot along the way. Me? I am an Ocean Girl, always have been, always will be. I was born with imaginary sand between my toes and salt water in my veins.

We were on our way to the Outer Banks of North Carolina and the Atlantic Ocean!

CHAPTER 38

RODANTHE, NORTH CAROLINA; CAPE HATTERAS, NORTH CAROLINA; AND VIRGINIA BEACH, VIRGINIA

You could smell it in the air: we were near the ocean! I rolled down the window and closed my eyes, enjoying the feel of warm air on my face, and pictured the perfect stretch of beach for an afternoon nap in the sun. With the exception of Galveston, we'd been land-locked for weeks. At last, we were heading towards the sea to the town of Rodanthe on the Outer Banks of North Carolina.

I vaguely remember the Nicholas Sparks book *Nights in Rodanthe*, which later became a movie with Diane Lane and Richard Gere— something about a woman, Inn-sitting in Rodanthe. Gere was the only guest, as a storm bore down on the Inn. I didn't see the movie or read the book, but somehow got an image of Rodanthe as a dark and stormy refuge for emotionally fragile people; I must have seen the trailer for the movie.

The real Rodanthe was anything but dark and stormy. I loved the beautiful beaches with fine-grain sand, warm breezes, and lack of tourists at that time of the year. We spent several days at a nice RV Park within walking distance of the beach and took full advantage of it, spending long afternoons on a blanket in the sand. Emmy even had her own beach umbrella! Watching her nap in the shade of her umbrella filled me with contentment and a sense of being present. It was the first time I'd seen east-coast sand dunes, covered in thick beach grass, and listing, sun-bleached, wooden fences to protect the dunes from two-legged and four-legged pedestrians. When she wasn't sleeping, Emmy was in her glory, running as fast as the wind and chasing sea gulls on long stretches of deserted beach. Every day we took our beach chairs to the edge of the surf and stared out over the horizon. Knowing we were staying in one place for a few days slowed down the pace. We spent hours in silent reflection at the water's edge. If this was a preview of what was to come, I was definitely in. I could have stayed on that beach for weeks, but we had other things to do.

Howard wanted to take the spiral staircase to the top of the 190-foot lighthouse on Cape Hatteras. I wished him Godspeed and waited at the bottom with Emmy. He has a little thing about heights, but it didn't stop him from scaling the lighthouse. When he got to the top, he put his hands on the railing and leaned forward so that I could get a picture with my telephoto lens. As I waited for him at the bottom near the entrance of the lighthouse, a woman appeared at the bottom of the stairs and made a shaky exit, falling into her friend's arms. I recognized her panic attack. Little did I know that the granddaddy of all panic attacks was waiting for me down the road.

It was very hot the day we visited the Kitty Hawk Memorial, our last stop in North Carolina. At Howard's urging, we walked from the two museums all the way to the memorial and back, about a mile round trip. Twice. I had a slight melt-down because there was a parking lot near the monument but (surprise) Howard wanted to walk rather than move the RV. In retrospect, it was worth it to see the site of the first successful flight in a heavier-than-air machine. Their flight took place on December 17, 1903—not all that long ago, when you think of how we take air travel for granted today. By the end of that day, both Emmy and I were exhausted. I was also slightly nauseated because I hadn't had enough water. I honestly can't remember if I sulked or complained or both, but I'm sure if you asked Howard he would be able to remember.

Virginia Beach, Virginia, was a different sort of treat with lots of restaurants and bars on the beach. Howard let me set the pace for our time in Virginia Beach, which meant we spent more time having drinks on a patio and sleeping on the beach, and less time walking around to see the sights. One night we had a wonderful dinner on the patio of a restaurant while Emmy slept underneath our table. It would have been perfect, except for the piercing burglar alarm that went off across the street right after our food arrived and didn't stop until we'd paid the bill and left the restaurant.

We spent several days in Virginia Beach being lazy tourists— bliss. The beach revived my spirits and soothed my monkey mind. The future felt limitless and brimming with possibilities. I was full of energy and wanted to ride that feeling for as long as possible.

The beautiful state of Virginia had a lot to offer. We visited Jamestown and Williamsburg, but decided to skip Yorktown. Two living history museums were enough—besides, we were going to tour James Monroe's farm in Charlottesville, just a mile from Monticello, Thomas Jefferson's estate; or as I referred to it, "Dead White Guys Old Houses." Our last stop in Virginia was Luray—not to be confused with Ouray, Colorado. Howard wanted to go down, down, down, into the caverns on a guided tour (again—not my cup of tea); he suggested that I spend an hour or two in the giant corn maze nearby while he was spelunking. Instead, I opted to check out the diner and read for a while. After coffee and a piece of pie, I went back to Sonward for a two-hour nap.

When I woke up, I felt disoriented and slightly jet-lagged from such a deep sleep in the middle of the day. I'd had a long dream about my mother and my daughter—something about Easter. I started to write it down, but the dream disappeared as quickly as smoke. For some reason, it seemed very important to remember it—like a little nudge from my subconscious—so I began writing in a stream-of-conscious way, hoping that the dream would return on its own.

I wrote about being a little kid and how Easter meant getting a collection of jellybeans, chocolates, and plastic eggs filled with surprises, all nestled in artificial grass on a paper plate. My father was not big on celebrations, so my mother walked a fine line between being able to express her nurturing spirit to her children, and having to deal with my father's anger or ridicule about spending money on foolish things. He mellowed considerably as he grew older, especially when grandchildren came along. He went from being the grumpy killjoy father, to a wonderful Opa who hid Easter eggs in the back yard for his young grandchildren.

I wrote about how I was a lot like my mother. We both saw holidays as an invitation to focus on something else for a change and a fine excuse to celebrate. It was my way to link to the past through rituals and traditions. Celebrating holidays was supposed to reinforce a sense of belonging and connection to family, but holidays could also bring out a primal sense of loss and melancholy.

I kept writing.

I wrote about being very young, and even then sensing that something important was missing in my small life, and how I'd been chasing it ever since. I didn't want that to happen to my daughter, yet as a single parent, I wasn't very good at being both mom and dad. What were the odds that she would have a hole in her heart, too?

I wrote that whatever was whispering to my heart was mine alone to hear, and that breaking into authenticity was strictly a one-woman act. If I were finally going to walk my own path, I would have to replace things that no longer served me: the need to please others, waiting for someone to read my mind rather than asking for what I needed, and spending my precious life nurturing an ungrateful spouse, boss, or friend, instead of my dreams.

Then it hit me: **I was the one who trained them!**

I trained Howard to expect my innate concern for his comfort as something normal to which he was entitled. Of course, he took my nurturing for granted. When it became a way of life, it stopped being special. A friend once told me that after she started working at Disneyland, she stopped seeing the magic and noticed the humidity.

What would happen if I thought about my needs and wants <u>first</u>? What if the only life I was responsible for was my own? What would I do *right now*, if I could do anything?

Maybe I'd bundle up and take the dog to the beach, along with my sketchpad, a few books, my favorite beach chair, and soft blankets. Perhaps I'd time-travel, and have brunch at that outdoor restaurant with the brick courtyard in Old Sacramento and listen to live jazz while sipping champagne. Maybe I'd go to church and begin to believe in hope and forgiveness again. After church, I'd put a ham in the oven before the kids and grandkids arrived. Better yet—I'd arrange flowers for the big dining room table that seated the entire family, and fill baskets with jellybeans, chocolates, and surprises for everyone. My hot husband would be in the back yard, getting the grill ready for dinner. Music would be playing.

As I wrote, I could see my mother smiling.

I wrote about how I used to load-up the car and head down the coast to my parents' house, almost 400 miles away. First stop: Santa Nella. Santa Nella was a pit stop for gas and food, about two hours south of Sacramento. It was also the home of Pea Soup Anderson's, a best friend to many travelers in California. Back in the day, you could get a bowl of soup, bread, and a drink for about a buck. Now, I think it is closer to $6—still a bargain, especially if you are hungry.

In addition to good food and a touristy gift shop, Pea Soup Anderson allowed local farmers to sell fresh fruits and vegetables in their large parking lot. We always stopped at their bakery for apple strudel, which my mom served with tea after dinner. After buying the strudel, we'd top-off the tank at the nearby Chevron. Years later, In N Out Burger would open down the road and cut into Pea Soup Anderson's business. No one—not even loyal Pea Soup Anderson customers—could resist the lure of a burger and fries from In N Out Burger. My daughter and I would start talking about it while we were still an hour away, so that by the time we got in line at the drive-through (there was always a long line), our mouths were watering and tummies growling.

The next stop was Pismo Beach. After five hours on the road, we were ready to stretch our legs on the beach for a while. Many years later, I would stop at Pismo Beach for lunch at The Tides restaurant on my way home to Sacramento. This had become my ritual after my mom got sick, when I drove back and forth to Lompoc. The Tides was my refuge, especially during her final days. I would stop there on my way to Lompoc to draw strength from the ocean as I sat on the deck and ignored the soup in front of me. I would stop again on the way home for a glass of wine, requesting the table closest to the water. It was then that I finally allowed myself the tears I'd been holding back during our visit; I never knew if our good-bye had been the last one.

I wrote about the early years when Lyndsay was little and we would visit Oma and Opa. After Pismo Beach, Lyndsay and I would stop in Morro Bay to play some more on the beach and work out my sore back and her wiggles. Morro Bay meant running on the beach, hunting for beach treasure, and a last chance to be noisy. It also meant that we were getting closer to my parents' house.

The last stop, of course, was Lompoc. The sheer joy on my mother's face upon seeing us was worth the trip. Even my dad, who rarely left his over-stuffed leather recliner in front of the TV, got up when we rang the doorbell to let us in. We would talk about traffic (none), the route (although it never deviated), and how the car was running (good—no complaints) before he'd wander off. My mother would be busy in the kitchen, but still plied us with offers of sandwiches to hold us over for an hour before dinner was ready.

I would throw our bags in the guest bedroom and join my daughter and mother in the kitchen to see if I could help with dinner. Lyndsay would already be wearing one of my mom's aprons, perhaps standing on a chair, depending on how old she was, and stirring something with a wooden spoon. My mom thought my daughter hung the moon, something that never failed to pull at something soft and vulnerable in my heart. As the visit stretched out over the next few days, my mom would spend uninterrupted hours with my daughter, something this single mom was not able to provide very often. She'd set up zip lines in the bedroom and fly stuffed monkeys from window to doorway. Other times, they'd play with toys from the closet that my mom kept full of garage sale treasures. She provided crayons, paper, and unconditional love to my child.

I wanted so badly to lift their disappointment in how my life had turned out. I never felt their judgment, but I knew they worried about me and how I would take care of a child alone, work full-time, and try to be happy. We had our rare moments, but everyone knew that it was very hard to be happy under the circumstances.

If our visit coincided with a holiday, the food preparations went into full gear. My brother and his wife would join us at the table with their three young children. When they were little, the cousins would play in the guest room—mostly my daughter and their son, who were three months apart in age—where my mom kept the toys. My brother and I would visit in the living room, as my mom sliced cucumbers in the kitchen. She refused help when offered. My mother always seemed happiest when she was feeding her family. I don't remember ever seeing her sit through an entire dinner. She was always hopping up to get more butter, fill someone's glass, or start the water for tea to accompany thick slices of angel food cake topped with strawberries from the farmer's market, and fresh (not canned) whipped cream. The biggest compliment you could pay my mother was to pat your bloated belly and groan with pleasure after one of her meals.

I had waves of mixed feelings during those visits, mainly because I could remember the times when our visits included Lyndsay's father, back when we were a "real" family. After the divorce, I felt like someone who had gotten off the bus at the wrong station in the middle of the night, and had to wait forever for another bus—all the while knowing it was never going to happen. The original destination had been leveled in a tsunami, lost in an earthquake, devoured by the flames of a lightning storm. I was grieving for a place that no longer existed, and maybe never had. I doubted that I would ever be happy again. I could always live wherever the next bus took me, but it would never be home.

At some point, Howard came back, raving about the caverns and asked me how I'd spent the afternoon. I told him I'd read for a while and then taken a nap. He didn't notice my swollen eyes.

Next destination: Washington DC.

CHAPTER 39

COLLEGE PARK, MARYLAND AND WASHINGTON DC

I had been to our country's capital several times, but always on business, never for pleasure. The first time I saw the White House was through the window of my taxi from the airport. Another taxi took me to a corporate event where we had cocktails on a rooftop venue near the White House. Our host had taken the trouble of setting up a telescope so that we could see what I assumed were Secret Service agents in black SWAT-type uniforms patrolling the perimeter of the White House roof. Were they looking at us at the same time?

I'd never been to Washington DC as a tourist, but that was about to change.

We found a great RV Park in College Park, Maryland, called Cherry Hill Park. It had every imaginable amenity, including a dog-walker for Emmy, a housekeeper for Sonward, and a bus stop at the entrance of the park. We used all of the amenities, especially the bus stop, for the next week. We'd get up early every morning, shower, eat breakfast, and then Howard would take Emmy for a long walk while I dried my hair, wrote in my journal, or read a book. I knew my serenity was short-lived and wanted to enjoy my time alone. I also knew that as soon as Howard and Emmy came back from their walk, it would be time to lace up my walking shoes and double-time it to the bus stop. No matter how early we left for the bus, we always seemed to be chasing it before the doors closed.

The bus took us to the transportation center where we caught the train into the city. Howard planned our daily itinerary with more sights than it was physically possible to see (or so I thought). We were on our feet for an average of 10 hours a day for a week straight. I developed a limp around day 3; my toes bled beneath the nail on day 5. I was falling apart! To this day, I have a dead zone on my left big toenail.

We did so much during that week—where to begin? Highlights include a rickshaw ride to Ford's Theater, site of President Lincoln's assassination, and the Lincoln Memorial. I had to smile at the Lincoln Memorial. Somehow, I thought we would have it all to ourselves—just like on TV commercials. I was shocked at the throngs of people jockeying for position to get their pictures taken in front of Mr. Lincoln's long legs. There were hundreds and hundreds of students of all ages with exhausted parents or chaperones in tow, which made me wonder if I would have appreciated it back in middle school (probably not).

We saw the original Constitution, the original Bill of Rights, all floors of at least five Smithsonian Institutes, and took a tour of the U.S. Capitol to see where Congress was supposed to be doing its job. With the exception of the rickshaw ride, we walked everywhere, backtracking often.

The part of the week that stands out the most for me is Arlington National Cemetery—624 acres of beauty and peace to honor soldiers, among others, who died while serving our country. There are over 14,000 veterans buried there, from as far back as the civil war, with more added every day (25-30 funerals are held *daily*).

In our misguided effort to find an exit, Howard and I stumbled upon a funeral in progress, and I couldn't help but weep as a horse drawn carriage bearing the casket passed. That was the second time that day I'd gotten emotional; the first was at the changing of the guard ceremony at the Tomb of the Unknown Soldier.

Once the casket had passed, the path was roped-off, including us among the funeral guests. We bowed our heads and tried to blend into the trees, not wanting to disturb the ceremony. My faded shorts were embarrassing, and I prayed that the family wouldn't notice or think I was being disrespectful. Howard and I were honored to bear witness to this timeless ritual. To imagine this ceremony repeated almost 11,000 times a year was staggering.

Arlington National Cemetery is also the final resting place of John F. Kennedy. I remember watching his funeral on TV when I was a kid, along with the rest of the country; the way the riderless horse pranced sideways; little John-John's salute; and the eternal flame at the grave. Now, here I was, standing in front of that eternal flame, absorbed in the wonder of being so close to JFK's tombstone. Just then, some asshole began talking loudly on his cell phone in front of the grave. Howard gave me his "leave it alone" look. This was not the place or the time for an ugly public scene. You dodged a bullet, Mr. Cellphone. Next time my husband may not be there to rein me in.

President Kennedy was not alone in the cemetery: two deceased Kennedy children were reburied in Arlington. In 1994, Jacqueline Bouvier Kennedy Onassis was buried next to President Kennedy. Howard's favorite Kennedy, Robert, was buried nearby in a simple grave, joined by a worn granite path to his brother's more elaborate resting place. "Just as he would have wanted it," Howard whispered.

It was impossible to see every monument and memorial in Arlington Cemetery. We saw only a fraction and promised ourselves we would come back for the rest.

Arlington's spiritual elegance against the obscenity of war and loss of life left us both stunned.

However, it wasn't all appreciation and reflection. At the end of each day, it was all I could do to slowly limp back to the subway station, tagging ten paces behind Howard, and ready to kill him if he suggested "just one more museum." On most days, we made our way through the itinerary and waited until we got home to eat dinner. After a while, my bloody toes and I simply could not keep up with Howard's 4 mph walking pace. I could handle sore legs and tried to ignore my aching feet, but I couldn't ignore the pain in my lower back. Walking briskly made everything ten times worse. Ironically, I was the one who blew through museums, studying exhibits that caught my eye and bypassing the rest, while my husband could easily spend up to 30 minutes in front of one display.

Between the humidity and the crowds, it didn't take long for us to start sniping at each other again. On good days, I realized that no one was right or wrong—we were just different. On bad days, I was convinced he was trying to kill me. It almost worked.

We had a disagreement one night after an exceptionally long day. We'd made a decision to find a place to eat dinner in town for a change, instead of heading back to the RV Park. There were plenty of restaurant options, but Howard wanted to see if there was a better restaurant "around the corner". This was an old dance: I was low on blood sugar and ravenous; he wanted to find the perfect place to eat. Of course we couldn't find a perfect restaurant (they were either too crowded or too empty, which made Howard suspicious) and ended up at Starbucks. I had visions of resting my feet in a restaurant with descent Italian food and maybe a nice bottle of Chianti; meanwhile, he was happy with a Vanilla Latte and a piece of frosted pound cake. To make matters worse, we snagged the only available outdoor table—right in front of a stinky bus stop, and next to a colorful street person who was drinking a can of beer out of a paper bag at the table next to ours. Naturally,

Howard noticed nothing out of the ordinary and finished his coffee while admiring the sunset in the distance, as I politely declined our neighbor's offer for a drink of his beer and inhaled bus fumes. We didn't speak the rest of the night.

Travel Tip: when a woman says she has to eat, she **HAS** to eat.

The next day we stopped early to attend a Washington Nationals baseball game. We rested our feet, drank beer, and ate hot dogs, while rooting for the home team. I don't remember who they played (I think it was San Diego), or who won, but my feet were grateful for the break. By the 7th inning stretch, we were friends again.

Our next stop included a few days in Annapolis, Maryland, touring the United States Naval Academy and sampling the local culture. I was beginning to realize (again) how often I had gone with the flow, especially when there was something else I really wanted to do. Why did I always defer to Howard's plans? I was going to have to retrain both of us if we were going to survive this trip.

There might have been more than one downtown (tourist vs. commerce), but for us, downtown Annapolis was a beautiful, seaside village in the shadow of the Naval Academy. On our way to the Academy, I saw Christmas ornaments in nautical themes through the window of a cute shop and wanted to take a closer look. My plan all along had been to pick up souvenirs along the way that would help us reminisce about the trip. But Howard was hell-bent on getting to the Naval Academy. He didn't want to miss the next tour, even though they had tours every hour on the hour. I suggested that we take a quick look. He promised me that we would stop in after the tour before we caught the bus back to the RV Park.

You guessed it: by the time the tour was over, and after walking all over hell's half acre looking at boats and buildings, we had just enough time to run to the bus stop to catch the last bus back to the RV Park. I was extremely disappointed and upset, but held my tongue while we were on the bus. In my state of mind, it was another sign that what I wanted wasn't important. I tried to calm down by taking long, slow, breaths, but it was no use.

Finally, in the privacy of the RV, I could no longer disguise my emotions, and asked if he knew why I was so upset. No idea was his response.

I was calm at first (or so I thought).

"Why didn't we go into that Christmas shop when I wanted to?"

"Here we go again," said Howard, ramping up for a tirade.

"Let me talk!" I said, a little louder.

He got louder, too. "I told you, we'd be late for the tour!"

"They. Had. Other. Tours." I was beginning to lose it.

"How was I supposed to know when the last bus left?" He was being deliberately obtuse.

"Goddammit, Howard. I really just wanted—"

"Why can't we just have a nice night? Why do you always dwell on shit like this? I'm trying to enjoy this trip but you're always ready to attack me. Why can't you let little things go?" I could tell he was really pissed off because he was pacing.

"BECAUSE IT'S NOT A LITTLE THING TO ME!"

"All this over a couple of Christmas decorations—we don't even have room for souvenirs!" He looked like he was about to head out the door.

"IT'S NOT JUST ABOUT THE SHOP! AND, IF I WANT A FUCKING SOUVINIR, I WILL BUY ONE AND FIND THE ROOM!" I was crying now.

"You want me to call you a cab, so you can go back and buy a plastic Santa? Fine. I'll call you a cab."

"I give up. You are missing the point. Besides, the shop closed an hour ago." But the bar is open, I thought to myself.

Howard just stood there with an exasperated smile on his face. It got ugly after that.

I stormed out in search of a restroom. By the time I got back, Howard had a baseball game on the satellite TV, as I rummaged around the refrigerator for the last of the bottle of wine we bought a week ago. I emptied what was left into a coffee mug and drank it while glaring at the back of his head.

Who was the crazy one, I wondered later, while smuggling Vodka into a glass of cranberry juice.

CHAPTER 40

OCEAN CITY, MARYLAND

Things went a little better at our next stop: Ocean City, Maryland.

Howard must have thought about what I said, because he found an RV Park on the ocean with its own Tiki Bar! We started drinking Mai Tai's at around 4:00. By 7:00, we were laughing with new friends and giving each other looks that said more than words could have. We had both behaved badly; it was time to put it behind us and have some fun.

Ocean City is the sister city to Sacramento. For years, I'd seen the signs on the freeway in Sacramento that read "Ocean City, 2862 miles". When we got to Ocean City, we saw the same sign in reverse. The Mai Tai's helped, but more than that, it felt great to be at the ocean again. The tension left my shoulders as we listened to stories from the locals, and took turns buying drinks. The next day, we took a walk on the famous Ocean City boardwalk. I tried Thrasher French fries, a local favorite, for the first time. Thrasher fries come in large servings; they have just the right amount of grease. The preferred way to eat them is with vinegar—yum! We ended the day with a nap on the beach and sunburns.

Life was very good that day. Howard was attentive, affectionate, and funny as hell, which made me wonder: Which was real—the people we became when we argued, or this great couple enjoying life on the beach?

To balance things out, we spent at least 1-2 nights in a hotel every week. Sonward was small and Emmy was furry, so it didn't take long for the dog hair, rough roads, and tight quarters, to grind on one or both of us. Staying in a hotel gave us a chance to spread out a little, take a real shower, and sleep in a real bed.

That's just what we did in Glen Burnie, Maryland, just before we caught an Orioles game at Camden Yards. After a long walk, Emmy settled down in our dog-friendly hotel room and we caught public transportation to the baseball game. I was quiet during the game and just wanted to blend in with the normal people around us. Truthfully, I was envious of their ability to go home to their own beds after the game, but sick of dwelling on it. I was determined to be more positive. I owed that to Howard.

CHAPTER 41

LANCASTER, PENNSYLVANIA

W e wanted to take the tour of an authentic Amish home, but struggled with whether or not it was respectful or exploitive. We had just arrived in Lancaster, Pennsylvania, after a night in Dover, Delaware, and tried not to stare at the horse-drawn buggies and simply dressed folks throughout the town. We saw strong, young boys riding stand-up plows through the fields, barefoot girls chasing horses that had escaped through a hole in the fence, and many identically dressed women walking with young children. Their way of life was so different from ours, it was hard not to stare and wonder if it a blessing to have your role so clearly defined since birth?

I'd read about Rumspringa, a rite of passage for 14-16 year olds, which enabled them to experience the non-Amish world before being baptized into the Amish community. There was an odd logic to forbidding almost everything outside the Amish community, and then allowing adolescents to date, watch TV, or even drink alcohol. If they came back to the community, they could do so without wondering what it was they were missing. They were somewhat allowed to question their beliefs *before* baptism, but afterwards—not so much.

We did end up visiting a working Amish farm and toured a typical Amish home model. The Amish tour guide even welcomed Emmy to accompany us on the tour and stopped to scratch her head often. Before our visit, I knew very little about them, beyond not using electricity (not always true) or buttons (true).

My respect for these gentle people grew throughout the afternoon. At first, I felt self-conscious about wearing modest shorts in the heat until I noticed other tourists in beer-themed tank tops, or visible bra straps.

Their lives were uncluttered in so many ways. Roles were well defined and critical to building a strong congregational community. We learned that there were different orders of the Amish. Each order is made up of congregations that have their own set of rules, known as Ordnung, that dictate their everyday life. That's why some Amish people are permitted to ride in cars, or use electricity to run machines in the barn, and others are not. People in the congregation take turns having church in their home every other week. The bishop is a member of the community without formal training and serves for life.

I couldn't imagine such a life of denial, but that didn't stop me from admiring their security, love, and work ethic.

I wasn't the only one with tears in my eyes when, in response to a question, our tour guide told the story of the Nickel Mines shooting.

On October 2, 2006, a non-Amish man shot 10 girls in a one-room schoolhouse in the Old Order Amish community of Nickel Mines in Lancaster County, Pennsylvania. The girls ranged in age from 6-13; five died. The shooter committed suicide at the scene. The reaction of the Amish community stunned the world when they offered love to the killer's family, and forgiveness for what he had done. Hours after the tragedy, an Amish neighbor visited and comforted his family to reassure them that forgiveness had already been granted by the families of the victims. Thirty members of the

Amish community attended his funeral, and they even set-up a charitable fund for the family of the shooter.

Amazing grace, indeed.

Although I couldn't afford a genuine Amish quilt ($600!), I left with an even better souvenir: knowledge, respect, and admiration for their way of life.

Our next stop could not have been further from the Amish community. Welcome to Hershey, Pennsylvania, for a tour of the Hershey Chocolate Factory. Then it was off to *Jim's Steaks* in Philadelphia, home of the best damn Philly cheesesteak sandwich in the world. Howard and I had a slight disagreement about seeing the Liberty Bell; it was getting late and we couldn't find a place to park. He wanted to see it. I wanted to skip it. We skipped it. We had miles to go before we slept, and there was a wicked thunderstorm on the way to our next stop: Atlantic City, New Jersey.

I was convinced that the worst was behind us. I should have known better.

CHAPTER 42
ATLANTIC CITY, NEW JERSEY

W e hit a new low a few days later...
On our way to Atlantic City, *To Sir with Love*, by Petula Clark, was blasting on the satellite radio. I seriously considered jumping out of the RV and into oncoming traffic when Howard began singing along at the top of his voice. I no longer kept track of good days or bad days; it was easier to accept that I was on a roller coaster. At that point of the trip, no matter how hard I tried, I couldn't shake the "black dog of depression outside my door," to quote Winston Churchill. I closed my eyes, plugged my ears, and tried to imagine a better future.

I am retired. I live in a nice house and take pride in my small garden. My backyard is a retreat, with shady places under big trees—perfect for curling up with a good book. I have a covered porch where I like to sit with a cup of tea when it's raining. My days are spent writing, volunteering, working in my garden, and cooking for my grandchildren during family visits. My needs, as well as most of my wants, are met. Every other month, I might take a trip for a weekend or so, but I'm always happy to be home again.

After pacing through smoky casinos in Atlantic City for two days, with all walks of life (some lower than others), we illegally spent the night *in the parking lot* of a casino, as drunks made their way to and from their cars all around us. It wasn't just the police and ambulance sirens throughout the night that got to me, it was also the suffocating humidity and sheer boredom of being in a place that held no interest whatsoever for me. I thought it would be different. The famous boardwalk overflowed with early morning drunks, sea gull shit, feral cats, one greasy taco truck after another, garish casinos, and sleazy t-shirt shops. One morning, I walked Emmy in a small patch of grass near one of the casinos, and startled when a deep voice in the bushes said hello. We had stumbled onto someone's encampment. Howard was playing in a marathon poker tournament as Emmy and I roamed the boardwalk in search of a place to pee.

I was still being tested, but not in my ability to camp for a year. That ship sailed long ago. I was being tested on how long I could continue to be a fish out of water. On good days, I counted the months until the trip was over. On bad days ... well, on bad days things got really rough.

CHAPTER 43

THE BREAKING POINT

It was the worst fight we'd ever had. The day after sleeping in the parking lot of the casino, we hit the road again and didn't speak for hours, except to yell at each other. It was Memorial Day weekend; I was worried about finding a place to stay that night. I wanted to start calling RV Parks, but Howard insisted that a spot would be available without advance reservations. I screamed at him inside my head about his magical thinking. Later, he got lunch for himself without asking me if I was hungry. To get back at him, I ignored his confusion about the toll roads. After 4 hours of driving through thunderstorms on rough stretches of highway that sent a shot of pain to my lower back with each pothole, we finally found at a campground in upstate New York that had an opening for $80 a night. There were hundreds of tents and RVs parked next to each other, with scores of noisy teenagers driving golf carts, and wild little kids riding their bikes on the one road leading in and out of the park. I hated my husband that afternoon, and I'm sure he hated me, too.

Once we hooked up the electricity and water, I desperately had to go to the bathroom. According to the map they gave us when we registered, it should have been just around the corner. I guess it was an old map. I finally found a restroom near the baseball field a half a mile away, where kids were playing a heated game. I felt nauseated from holding it in for so long and ran to the nearest stall, only to be confronted by the putrid odor of seeping mold and years of neglect—and worse. I was desperate. I hovered over the filthy toilet and tried to hold my breath when I wasn't gagging, as the first wave of explosive diarrhea hit.

Physically weak and looking for a fight, I made my way back to Sonward. The humidity was overwhelming, as were the mosquitos. When I got back to the RV, I sprayed Emmy from head to tail with bug spray. Howard was gone. I found out later that he'd gone to the office to see about another space because our camping spot was in the trees, making reception for the satellite dish impossible. We ended up moving to the over-flow area, a field near the noisy swimming pool, and a long walk to the restrooms. We still weren't speaking as Howard watched golf on TV for a few hours. I had nothing but dark thoughts and decided to go for a walk.

I could no longer see beyond the cramped quarters, constant togetherness, and lack of control over our itinerary. Life was too short for this bullshit.

The day before was the anniversary of the death of my oldest friend's only child, Adam. She and I met decades earlier when we were both married and 9 months pregnant. Our kids were born within a week of each other and grew up thinking they were siblings because we spent so much time together—especially later, when we were both single mothers. His murder was devastating. While Howard was playing in his poker tournament in Atlantic City the night before, and I was in the RV with Emmy, the anniversary hit me. I looked on the Internet for an update into the investigation and read about two men who were on trial for Adam's murder. Our problems were so trivial compared to this tragedy. Trite, but true: there were no guarantees, life was short, and it could change in an instant.

I was wasting my life, but rather than do something about it, I blamed fear, procrastination, and Howard.

That was the common thread in almost all of my journal entries. I'm still doing an old dance dating back to my childhood, when my mother would focus on the worst-case scenario to keep us safe. In her world, the boogeymen were real during the war, and anticipating the worst helped her survive. She taught us always to be on the alert for danger lurking in even the most innocent places; I was a good student. Protection against the "what-ifs" became second nature to me by the time I was old enough for school. Vigilance was exhausting.

I *can't* be the only one. How many times have you heard, "don't get too happy, because it may fall apart," from a well-meaning friend? Or wondered when the other shoe would drop after something good happened? Let's not forget my personal favorite—resolving to be happy "later." I was always going to be happy *after* my first husband finished college, when it would be my turn; *after* my daughter's dad and I finally settled our divorce; *after* I wasn't busy at work anymore. I was still doing it—delaying happiness until *after* the trip and we found a new home; or *after* we learned to get along better and fight fair. Adam's murder proved there might not be an *after.*

I found my way back to the RV. To soothe myself (and punish him), I started drinking. I couldn't spend another night in the silence of his judgment and disappointment. We were only four months into a yearlong trip and our marriage was in real trouble. I wanted to talk to Howard—I *needed* to talk to him—but I was afraid it would escalate into another argument, and I didn't have it in me anymore. I desperately needed to talk to my best friend (Howard) and find comfort in his arms, but I knew that was probably impossible. We had fallen too far. When I finally did try to talk to him, it came out all wrong. Instead of tenderness, I challenged, and then demanded, that he to talk to me. The wine had been a mistake. When he ignored me, I lost it. I didn't think I could feel any worse but I was wrong.

That's when the mother of all panic attacks started.

My heart began racing. My palms were sweaty and cold. I was terrified; I couldn't breathe. Every inch of my body was screaming at me to run. I had to get out of that RV immediately—my life depended on it. I had to get out. I had to get out. I had to get out. Where were my keys? I started looking through drawers and cupboards for my car keys, not realizing that they would do me no good. I had no car. I had no house. I didn't need keys. I needed my purse, shoes, credit cards and cash. Howard finally looked up from the TV and got a worried look on his face. He tried to calm me down—fail. He tried to put his arms around me—fail. He told me to stop looking for keys, purse, money—fail. I was in full survival-mode.

I would run as fast as possible. I would somehow find my way to JFK airport, and fly away from this awful place. I had to run or I would die.

Howard had tears in his eyes as he blocked the door to make sure I couldn't get out.

CHAPTER 44

AFTERMATH – A FORK IN THE ROAD

The next morning, I was still in the RV. I woke up with swollen eyes from crying, and a wicked hangover. Slowly, the memory of last night came back. When Howard came back from walking Emmy he wouldn't look at me or talk to me, except to say that the trip was over—we would head back to California tomorrow because he knew I would never be happy otherwise. I briefly wondered how often he would throw this in my face during future arguments, until I realized that there might not be any future arguments.

We might never recover from this trip.

I flashed back to the night before, struggling in vain to get out the door, as his eyes filled with tears.

"I can't let you go—don't you know that? It makes no sense. How could you even consider doing this to me? Do you know how worried I would be, not knowing where you were, or whether you were safe? Do you have any idea of what that would do to me?" He kept pleading for me to stay put.

Things looked different the next morning. I was filled with regret for being a bad travel partner, for not being able to see what a bucket-list prize I'd been given, for all the times I knew he bit his tongue during one of my meltdowns. I was losing a truly good man whose unspeakable crime was modeling how to live your dreams and see the positive in everything and everyone.

I was filled with regret, because I'd known all along—before we took a step out of town, before we bought Sonward, before we turned in our retirement papers, and during all the times we talked to friends about our big adventure—that it wasn't for me. I set the stage to be snowballed into something that had a high risk for failure all *because I was afraid of the consequences of telling the truth.*

There it was again—fear. Fear of losing him if I hadn't gone along, fear of regret if he didn't get to finish this trip, fear of his resentment. I have been living with fear and shame just beneath the surface of my skin and counting the rows to the exit for as long as I can remember. I have used humor, sarcasm, and anger, to disguise my deep fear. My pattern had been one of running-running-running every few years, changing my name, changing my preferences to better fit with whoever I was in love with at the time, and *changing my dreams to match those of my partner's.*

It was all a waste of time because it didn't keep me safe! I still got divorced, still got hurt, still felt lost. If I hadn't abdicated responsibility for my life to others, I may have found myself in a very different place—not better or worse—just different. At least I would have no one but myself to blame.

I was sick inside, tired, embarrassed, humiliated, and so, so, sorry. Howard and I were through talking.

However, as we began packing for the trip back to California, a new feeling began to emerge. The worst had happened—I'd lost him—and I was still standing. It was then that I knew I would be okay. I was a survivor. On some level, I knew the problem had not been the road trip or his annoying habits (okay, maybe a little). I knew the problem was that *I had not been living the life I wanted, and blamed everyone else except the one person who had the power to make that happen: me.*

In that broken moment, when all hope should have been lost, a better hope began to emerge.

I'd wasted years in therapy to deal with anxiety and depression while the answer was right there in front of me. Like Dorothy in Oz, I'd had it all along.

After our blow-up on Memorial Day in that crowded RV Park with the mosquitoes, the crazy kids, too much alcohol, too much stimulation, and too much togetherness, I knew I had crossed the line and he was as good as gone, but I wasn't ready to give up yet. We'd come too far to turn back now. I knew if we went back to California, our marriage would have no chance of healing. We had to continue a little farther down the road—I had never been surer of anything in my life. It was finally time to tell him exactly what I wanted and needed.

What I said next shocked both of us.

I wanted to go to Cape Cod and Martha's Vineyard before we went back to California to deal with what I was sure would be another divorce under my belt. I had no home, no transportation, no job, and in all likelihood, no husband. But I wanted to see Cape Cod. If he didn't want to go with me, I was going to go without him. I had no idea how I would make any of that happen, but I knew I wouldn't go back to California without seeing the color of the sky on the Cape.

Thank God, he agreed.

CHAPTER 45
CAPE COD, MASSACHUSETTS

The moment we got to the other side of the Sagamore Bridge, I felt the air change. It was hard to see anything beyond the dense trees on either side of Route 6.The clouds were starched white against a deep blue sky with a touch of purple in it. We hadn't said much to each other since Memorial Day, but it was a different kind of silence. Neither of us was sulking. We were both grieving and tender towards each other during those times when we had to interact. These could be our last days together, and we knew it.

The same fist in my heart that let go long enough to go to Pebble Beach a hundred years ago, released its grip on me again while on we were on Cape Cod. There was a very real chance that we would be separating in California, but for now, I felt like I was home. I would deal with everything else later.

After getting settled in a beautiful RV Park in Falmouth with tall trees, an adults-only swimming pool, kayak rentals, and golden silence (not a kid in sight), we took a drive to see if we could find a nice place for dinner. At last, we were going to see beyond the trees.

I don't know if I wept from relief or fatigue, but the first time I saw a small white cottage with bright red Geraniums in a glazed, dark blue pot on the front porch, I lost it. **I have been writing about this place all of my life, but I never knew it had a name**. I saw my dream cottage on the main road, down narrow side streets, and around every turn. I couldn't look away. By the time we got to the Flying Bridge restaurant for dinner, I was a mess. We ate outdoors on the patio and watched as the boats gently swayed in the harbor. I devoured a boiled lobster dinner with a hunger I hadn't felt in a very long time and looked at my husband with love and gratitude. Our marriage was still up in the air, but he was the one who brought me to this magical place, and for that, I was grateful. I was finally living in the moment.

It felt like home.

After dinner, we walked up and down the streets of Falmouth like a couple of kids in Disneyland. Cape Cod blew Howard away, too. We took it all in—the small shops, restaurants, bakeries, day spas, 100+ year-old churches, and dogs. Dogs were everywhere! Emmy would love living here. A new thought began to take hold in my heart. Was my intuition speaking to me?

If our marriage was truly over, this is where I would live.

After less than 24 hours, I was ready to leave everything behind in California and live on Cape Cod. I imagined my daughter flying out several times a year, friends visiting, and going back to California for periodic visits. Cape Cod was where I wanted to plant my new flag. I felt as strongly about this as I had when I was much younger, and knew I had to get out of Lompoc. However, this time I would be running towards something, not away from it.

We made it back to the RV Park a little after the sun had set, and took Emmy for a walk to the lake where a dozen colorful kayaks were tied up for the night. We passed the usual RVs and tents, and a few small modular homes where people lived year-round, or so we thought. There is no such thing as a year-round RV Park on the Cape—they officially close for the winter on October 15, and open again April 15. Unbeknownst to me, this planted a seed in my husband's head.

We spent the next week exploring from one end of the Cape (Buzzard's Bay) to the other (Provincetown). We actually checked out a small cottage on the beach that was for sale. It was a 1-bedroom, 1-bathroom, 400 square foot cottage with a small loft, tiny bathroom, kitchen, and outdoor deck with killer views of the sunset—all for $40,000. Did I mention that it was fully furnished, too? That was the good news. The bad news was, you had to pay $8000 a year in maintenance fees and could only live there from April through October.

Next came a beautiful drive on Highway 6a, but do not let the name fool you. Highway 6a is a two-lane road that passes through quintessential Cape Cod towns and villages—if you want speed, take Highway 6 instead.

It was sweltering hot when we drove Sonward into Provincetown—known locally as P-town. We could barely navigate down the narrow streets, so we parked Sonward, put a leash on Emmy, and took a walking tour of the first place the Pilgrims landed before saying *to hell with this, it is too cold here and the soil is too sandy—let's go to Plymouth.* We ate a lobster roll, walked the full length of Main Street, and peeked into touristy shops before heading to a dog-friendly beach and soaking up even more sun.

It felt so good to be comfortable in my skin again. I loved everything about Cape Cod; I felt more relaxed there than anywhere else in the world. Then it hit me—Cape Cod was *my* dream—it was no wonder I felt at home. Now I knew how Howard felt about this trip, and I nearly doubled-over at the realization that I had ruined it for him.

It was early June. We had already stayed on the Cape longer than we planned and soon it would be time to go. But we were no longer talking about California. We decided to extend our time on the east coast by taking advantage of our proximity to Canada and visit the North Atlantic Provinces. We had two days left to explore the rest of the Cape. I tried to ignore the pain in my stomach at the thought of leaving.

No. No more ignoring my feelings and suffering in silence.

"I could live here … and I'm heartbroken about leaving," I told Howard.

"I know, baby," he said quietly, and squeezed my hand.

The next day he spent a lot of time on the laptop. When I asked him what he was doing, he was evasive. Several hours later, he called me over to check out what he had found on Craigslist.

It was a beautiful 2000 square foot, two-story Cape Cod style house for rent in the small village of Cotuit (population around 2500), mid-way between Falmouth and Hyannis. It was fully furnished and a very short walk to the water. The back yard butted-up to a 97-acre preservation area. It would be available from Labor Day until the middle of May next year.

"Wanna go see it?" he said with a smile.

CHAPTER 46
"OH, CANADA ..."

We spent the rest of June, July and August on the road, working our way up the east coast with stops in Maine: first, Kennebunkport ("best damn lobster rolls in the world" and home to the family compound of George H.W. Bush), and a week at dog-friendly Old Orchard Beach. Camden, Rockland, Bar Harbor, and Bangor, were next. We had a luxurious couple of nights at the Hartstone Inn, a dog-friendly B&B with gourmet meals and a very friendly staff, before heading north to Canada.

We made it through Customs with no drama—not yet, anyway. We were about 3 miles into Canada when I felt another panic attack coming on. What the hell? I turned on my Kindle, hoping to distract myself by downloading a new book, but no luck. I couldn't get reception. Howard was trying to drive and read the roadmap (our Garmin was for the U.S. only). He pulled over and, just as quickly, a car pulled up and stopped next to us. My old fear about being murdered by the side of the road added to the rising panic attack, as a man motioned for Howard to roll down the window. I almost screamed *Nooooooooo!* Good thing I didn't because this very nice man noticed we looked confused and wondered if maybe he could be of assistance. Welcome to Canada.

We spent about 10 days in Canada. Highlights include the Bay of Fundy, where the tides go out thousands of feet several times a day. Boats perched and listing on dry rocks in the morning float in 60 feet of water by afternoon. At night, we watched lighted Japanese lanterns lift out over the ocean, and drank beer with the locals. We spent the Fourth of July in an RV Park overlooking the ocean.

Our first stop was at St. Martins in New Brunswick, and later, Moncton, home to a dog-friendly Casino/Hotel, which we visited twice, one upon entering Canada and once upon leaving. Then it was on to the quiet beauty and isolation of Prince Edward Island (home and final resting place of *Anne of Green Gables'* author Lucy Maud Montgomery), where we stayed in Cavendish. Finally, it was on to Halifax and Nova Scotia before re-entering the good old U.S. of A.

I learned so much while we were in Canada, such as:

I have an ancient Kindle, which only works in the U.S. Next time I will download a ton of books before crossing the border. I learned that I watch too much TV, read too many Stephen King books, and have a very active imagination. Not all strangers are out to kill you—some just want to help you when you're lost.

Looking back, I think the panic attack after crossing the border into Canada was rooted in two things: being in a different country without the tether of a home, and not knowing if we would still be married in a year. The only other time I had felt that threatened was at the airport in Naples, Italy, where uniformed security guards carried machine guns.

It was no longer acceptable to be hard-wired to look for threats at the expense of missing the beauty of the moment.

I also learned that I can be still and study tide pools while my husband goes for a power walk without feeling resentment or guilt.

Finally, I learned that Canadians (in addition to being very generous souls) are funny as hell. We met locals with a great sense of humor and even greater capacity for kindness. I may have entered the country with trepidation, but I left with a full heart, sore legs from hiking, and a lifetime of memories.

Soon, it was time to go back to America.

But first, Emmy scared the hell out of me while we were in Moncton. Although the casino/hotel was dog friendly, they forgot to charge us the $50 per day pet fee upon check in. Had I learned nothing about integrity? I should have insisted that we march down to the front desk and correct the error. Instead, we let it ride. That meant I had to sneak her past the front desk every time she needed a potty-walk. I know, I know, they had no way of knowing that we didn't pay the pet fee, but have you not read the last hundred pages? I simply cannot pull off a poker face.

On one of our clandestine trips through the lobby with the marble floor, Emmy suddenly sat down and refused to move. She only did this when she had either to (a) throw up or, (b) take a shit now— not ten seconds from now — right *now*. I could already sense people staring at us and didn't want to find out if she was going with (a) or (b), so I began to drag her by the leash towards the front door. She stood up abruptly, trying to cooperate, but couldn't find traction on the marble floor, so down she went again—this time splayed out in the middle of the lobby, just as the elevator opened and 4 women in housekeeping uniforms rushed over to help. We were officially a spectacle. Poor baby—it was (b) after all. We survived our adventure in the lobby and she got lots of Beggin' Strips to make up for putting her in such a bad position.

We still had our Canadian accents as we stopped in Augusta, Maine, for gas. As Howard filled the tank with gas, I filled my Kindle with books. After a week in the quiet solitude of Canada, it was back to the noisy crowds in Walmart, where we stopped for supplies. Life was much easier in Canada because we didn't have 100 choices for toothpaste and you bought fruit and produce because it was in season, rather than choose from a bounty of fruit from South America. Still, it was good to be back. Even Emmy looked like she felt better on U.S. soil.

Next stop: Cooperstown, NY, The Baseball Hall of Fame (during the Cincinnati Reds great Barry Larkin, and Chicago fan-favorite, Ron Santo, induction).

We left Emmy in the air-conditioned RV while we spent the afternoon at the Baseball Hall of Fame. She joined us for dinner on the deck of a nearby restaurant while we talked about how far the three of us had come in almost 6 months.

Our good friends Elliot and Kathie were going to meet us at Niagara Falls (insert Marx Brothers routine here) and we had many things to look forward to over the next few days. Life was beginning to feel normal again.

The night before we crossed the border again into Canada to meet Elliot and Kathie, we stayed in a great RV Park that had both a wine tasting at night, and a pancake feed in the morning. It wasn't until we were getting ready to leave that I got a sinking feeling; we were carrying contraband that could land us in prison. When we left Canada the first time, a border patrol agent actually came on board to check for fruits and vegetables after we told him that we had none. I had forgotten about the tomato in the vegetable drawer of the refrigerator. He scolded us and said that we were lucky; the other agents would have fined us $500 for not declaring that tomato.

This time, it wasn't a tomato: we had a can of Mace and a mini stun gun for security. We weren't about to carry a gun on our trip, but we needed more than a big stick if someone broke in while we were sleeping.

I looked it up online and learned that both items were illegal to carry into Canada. You could buy them there, but you couldn't transport them in. What to do?

Howard had a quiet conversation with the RV Park manager and came back saying it was going to be okay. The park was so close to the border that the manager was used to stupid people like us needing a place to stash their contraband. He was happy to hold our Mace and Zapper in a Tupperware container sealed with Duct tape until we could pick it up on the way back.

We didn't realize how much we missed our friends until we spent two days with Elliot and Kathie. Elliot, Kathie, and Howard, who used to work together, were catching up on office gossip. Kathie and I had a lot in common, too. We had both been single mothers and had both recently remarried. I *loved* having another woman to talk to and kept things light. After we said good-bye to Elliot and Kathie, we went to a different Falmouth—this one in Michigan, to visit dear friends, Jim and Christine.

CHAPTER 47

FALMOUTH, MICHIGAN

Jim and Christine live in a beautiful home that Jim built on 40 acres in the middle of some of the prettiest country you will ever see. Emmy was in her glory. When she wasn't sleeping on the porch, she was on alert for deer and squirrels. There is something very special about seeing your dog run across an open field without wearing a collar or dragging a leash.

We were staying in the small stone house that Jim's grandfather built at the front of the property. When Jim was a child, his whole family lived in that tiny house. Once Jim finished building the new house in the back of the property, Christine converted the stone house into a furnished guesthouse, complete with an ever-present plate of freshly baked cookies on the kitchen table. Jim and Christine's house was 2,000 feet from the stone house, with a well-worn path through the field connecting the two. Jim was waiting on the porch of "our house" when we arrived.

We had met Jim and Christine earlier through our kids, and became instant friends. Howard and I felt completely inept around them, because Christine knew how to can the bounty of her garden, cooked amazing meals, made butter, refinished furniture, sewed, knew how to build a house—you name it, she could do it.

Jim was a mystery. How could one man have so many skills and such talent? He builds things, invents things, modifies things, buys broken things and fixes them good as new, and plays a mean guitar. Like I said, Howard and I felt completely and lovingly inept (and in awe) around them.

Take dinner on our first night, for example. Christine made a smoked pork roast, served with jars of beets and green beans (which she'd put up last year), homemade buttermilk biscuits, and oh, yeah—homemade coconut pie for dessert. She wouldn't let me help with the clean up after dinner, so I sat on a bar stool and kept her company while she loaded the dishwasher. Howard and Jim played Cribbage nearby on a Cribbage board that Jim *made by hand*, as a gift for Howard. Christine gave me a beautiful German teacup and saucer that she found at a garage sale and said it reminded her of me. One night, Jim pulled out his guitar (he makes those, too) and played songs from the 70s while we sang along; we even got a 3-part harmony going during *Our House*, by Crosby, Stills, Nash and Young. It felt good to be around them.

Three days later, we said our sad good-byes and hit the road again. We were on our way back to Kansas City, where I would get on an airplane to visit my daughter for her birthday. Howard and I were both looking forward to some alone time. It didn't take long to resort to our old dysfunctional road behavior, but this time we managed to put things into perspective and tried harder.

After a drive that was too long, with too-little food, we bickered on the way to Kansas City. I unbuckled my seat belt and retreated to the couch to read my Kindle for the remainder of the day as Howard drove through the rain. That was the same day that a tour bus hit a bridge pillar on I55 near Litchfield, Illinois; one woman was killed and over two dozen people injured. We were tied up in traffic for hours, but in spite of the frustration, we kept quiet and let the anger of the day ebb away.

I was learning that it was not necessary to talk everything out. Sometimes you just have to write it off as a bad couple of hours. Besides, I was going to Lake Tahoe to spend a long weekend with my daughter for her birthday. I couldn't wait to take a walk along the lake. I also couldn't wait to be in California again.

This was not the first time I'd left the road for a short break. Back in March, my good friend, Barbara, called to invite me to Miami Beach for a long weekend in July with her and some of my favorite friends from work. They were going to be at a sales meeting for most of the week, but had extended the hotel reservation (Ritz Carlton!) after the meeting, and wanted to know if I would join them. The company had negotiated a great price on a huge suite, which Barbara offered to share with me. All I would have to pay for was airfare. I declined at first, but then I realized that a long weekend in Miami with my girlfriends might be just what this road-weary traveler needed.

Howard dropped me off in the rain at the airport in Detroit and I landed in Miami a few hours later to brilliant sunshine and a pitcher of Margaritas at the Ritz. The gang and I spent our first day in a private cabana with endless cocktails and gossip until the sun went down. Then it was out on the town for dinner and more cocktails. We spent most of the next day reading by the pool and talking. At one point, a pool attendant stopped by to ask if anyone wanted sunscreen. Thinking he was passing out samples, I said sure. The next thing I knew, he whipped out a can of refrigerated sunscreen and began spraying it all over my body. I screamed as it hit my hot skin—so much for staying undercover. I forgot all about life on the road and reveled in the company of good friends, good food, and world class accommodations. Ol' Sonward was going to be hard to get used to again after a suite at the Ritz. That was at the end of July.

It was now early August and, once again, I would be getting on an airplane. The plan was that I would meet Howard and Emmy in Austin, Texas, after visiting my daughter for her birthday, just in time for his daughter's college graduation and baby shower.

While I was visiting Lyndsay in California, Emmy got very sick in Austin. At first, Howard downplayed her condition over the phone because he knew I would be worried. When he finally told me about her symptoms, they sounded heat-related, so I encouraged him to put her in a cold tub of water and keep her in the air-conditioned house. No walks in the Texas heat—well over 100 degrees on most days. He called again later that night to say she had stopped eating and had spent the day sleeping. Now I was worried—especially when he didn't answer his phone the next day. I had no way of knowing that he was busy taking her first to the Vet, and then to an emergency animal hospital in Austin, after waking up in the middle of the night and finding her unresponsive.

The three of us were a pack! We had been through so much—traveling together, eating together, sleeping together, and braving all the forces of nature together. We had done everything to keep her healthy, comfortable, and safe. I even put a sweater and socks on her when we were going over Stevens Pass in Washington, because the floor of the RV felt cold. I kept reviewing her environment to see if I'd missed anything. She had her own bed, complete with thick insulation, and her little stuffed dog for company. We hired dog sitters and dog walkers if we were going to be gone a long time. We always kept the air conditioner or heat going so she could nap in comfort while we were gone. Howard was great about taking her for long walks every day. I carried her vaccination papers with us so we could get her groomed while on the road (reputable groomers will not touch a dog without proof of vaccinations). Yes, she was almost 12 years old, but you'd never know it to see her run through the open fields at Jim and Christine's, stare down a herd of deer, chatter at prairie dogs, bound through the snow, join us in bed with big eyes during thunder storms, and wait out a tornado watch! This was our Emmy—our traveling buddy. She couldn't die—not now. Not while I was so far away.

Of course, I didn't know the true extent of her condition until I finally got to Austin. It took several more days, but she slowly came back, after hand feeding her and offering sips of water every hour on the hour. We would learn later that her food was at fault.

We usually bought a large 40-lb. bag of dog food (the good stuff - $$$) and stored the open bag in the small bathtub of the RV, with the top clipped shut. Texas is always hot during the summer but in 2012, it was exceptionally hot. Nowhere on the bag does it say to store the food in a cool place, and there were certainly no warnings about excessive heat. Suspecting a bad batch of dog food, we stopped at a national pet store chain and told them our story to see if there had been a recall. It turned out that the chemistry of the dog food changed due to extreme temperatures inside the parked RV. The food literally baked and became toxic. Another lesson learned.

After Danielle's college graduation (at eight months pregnant!) and subsequent celebration party, it was time to head east again.

It wasn't long before we found ourselves in Oklahoma City, at the site of the Oklahoma City National Memorial, where a massive explosion occurred at 9:02 in the morning on April 19, 1995. The suspect, Timothy McVeigh, was later convicted of detonating a rental truck full of explosives in front of the Alfred P. Murrah Federal Building and killing 168 people—some of whom were children at the on-site day care center. Both the interactive museum and the outdoor memorial were stunning in their poignancy.

Howard put the pedal to the metal as we journeyed further north to Fargo, North Dakota, where we visited the Roger Maris Museum in the West Acres Shopping Center in Fargo, North Dakota. Roger Maris is famous for breaking Babe Ruth's single-season home run record, when Maris hit 61 home runs in 1961. Why a shopping mall? Maris was a very humble person. He preferred that they "put it where people will see it and where they won't have to pay for it." The museum is open every day except Christmas Day, Easter, and Thanksgiving. We followed-up the museum visit with a quick stop by Maris' grave at the Holy Cross Catholic Cemetery, also in Fargo. People had left small tokens—coins, miniature baseball bats, candles, flowers—on Maris' headstone as a way to show respect. I smiled when I found a rock that had the word "Fran" engraved on it and showed it to Howard. His mother's name was Fran, and it seemed fitting to acknowledge another coincidence.

Bloomington, Minnesota, is the home of the Mall of America—over 96 acres of stores, restaurants, theme parks with roller coasters, and even an Aquarium with over 4,000 sea animals. We didn't begin to scratch the surface of the 530 retail stores poised to gladly take our money. I was exhausted just walking from the parking area to the entrance!

It was after a long day at the Mall of America that we received a phone call with sad news: Howard's cousin (and one of his favorite people) had passed away in Long Island, New York. We had to drive from Minnesota to New York for the funeral. It was too late to go shopping for appropriate funeral clothes by the time we pulled into Long Island, so we attended in our best casual clothes. We barely made it.

A few days after the funeral, we decided to visit Bethel, New York, the site of the iconic Woodstock Music Festival, which took place back in 1969. I was halfway expecting to see a lake of mud, naked people romping in the woods, and many outhouses. Instead, we saw beautiful rolling hills covered in lush, green grass. In addition to a plaque commemorating Woodstock, they also had a very cool (or should I say groovy?) museum on the grounds, with lots of interesting exhibits and memorabilia. We spent over 3 hours there and could have stayed much longer if it were not for the Stone Temple Pilots concert that night at the Bethel Woods Center for the Arts. We got great seats and bragging rights for having attended a concert at Woodstock. The ghosts of our youth were all around ("Watch out for the brown acid, man.").

It took about 10 days from the time we left Austin, before we pulled into our campground in Falmouth, Massachusetts, where my husband finagled the only spot with TV reception by telling the office that his wife had a disability and had to be near the restrooms. He 'fessed up after I made a comment about how the office staff looked at me funny when I went in for change for the Laundromat.

No matter—we were back on Cape Cod!

CHAPTER 48

BIG SURPRISE!

Yup. Back in June, we signed the lease for the house in Cotuit and now we still had a few days before we could move in on Labor Day! My husband was my hero. Our marriage had been on the brink, when he saw the longing in my heart for a home on the Cape. We had to pass an interview with the owners—a very nice couple that used the house during the summer and rented it out during the off-season. They were interviewing one other couple but, fortunately, Bob (the owner) said he was a baby-boomer, too, and said we had to stick together.

I cried when his wife, Trisha, called to say that the house was ours.

I couldn't believe it! I'd been writing about this place for years. Back in the early 1980s, I wrote a short story about my imaginary 1000 square foot cottage, with its wide porch and stunning views of the water. When temperatures hit over 100 degrees for days on end back when I lived in Sacramento, I wrote about beaches that were longer than they were wide. During bouts of insomnia, in the quiet of the late-late night, I wrote about curling up in an Adirondack chair with sun-bleached pillows, and reading on the covered porch while sheets of rain came down.

I wrote about moving the kitchen table outdoors for clambakes during the summer; filling glass jars with wild flowers; and sweeping sand off the porch before my guests arrived for dinner. I wrote about riding my bike to the village in the morning for coffee, walking the dogs, and then sitting down to write for hours at a time. I wrote about how the light changed throughout the day, from impossibly blue, to a swirl of fire at sunset. I wrote as though this place already existed in the future and was patiently waiting for me to come home.

Now we were actually going to live there!

The house came with kayaks, fishing poles, bicycles, golf clubs, and clam rakes. There were Japanese Maples in the front yard and Hydrangeas in the back. There was even a trail from our back yard to the Nantucket Sound. Our house was set back in the woods but still very near the ocean. My shoulders dropped and I could breathe freely again. It was everything I had ever wanted, and more.

Howard had given them our deposit back in June—the place was ours until May 15! We unloaded our clothes, bedding, towels, and Emmy's blankets and toy. The house came with everything we would need, right down to the ceramic platter for our Thanksgiving turkey. It took all of 20 minutes to move in.

The first thing we did was take Emmy for a walk around our new neighborhood. Although we had neighbors on two sides, the trees provided more than enough privacy, we felt alone in the silent woods. We were about 5 miles from the nearest large grocery store, if you didn't count the Cotuit Market, a tiny mom-and-pop store with a deli and great wine selection. We noticed something else about the neighborhood: everyone waved. There were simply no strangers in Cotuit, and I think we got extra street-cred for renting during the off-season instead of the summer like most tourists (especially a few months later, when Hurricane Sandy blew through). If a car passed while we were walking the dog, the driver waved every time. Soon, we were the first to wave.

It was a two-story house. The master bedroom and bathroom, as well as the living room, dining room, kitchen, second bathroom, laundry room and guest room, were all downstairs. It had a huge deck along the back of the house, complete with a barbeque, outdoor dining area and bench seating. We also had an enclosed all-weather room. During the summer, the room had screens, during the winter, glass.

The second floor had another full bathroom, linen closet, two regular bedrooms, and a very wide bedroom that the owners referred to as "the dorm," because you could fit several beds next to each other and sleep another 6-8 kids in there. That was the only room they kept locked, because they used it as storage for their personal items. The two regular bedrooms upstairs each had their own deck overlooking the woods with a glimpse of the bay. We took a quick peek at the spooky (to me) basement and I decided it would be best not open that door too often. The house also had an outdoor shower, and small shed which held the bikes, etc.

Unless we had company, we could live exclusively downstairs.

No clandestine dog for our new home: we were up front about having a Golden Retriever, even though the ad said no pets. Bob said he loved Goldens and had no problem with Emmy. Without even meeting our dog, he approved her on the spot.

It was a new beginning, but it was also an ending: no more public bathrooms! No more hand dryers, aka puffs of warm air designed to get you to wipe your hands on your pant legs. No more misty showers with water-saving nozzles (how's a girl to rinse her delicate parts when, like Hawaiian rain, the water evaporated before hitting anything below shoulder-level?). No more avoiding eye contact with the woman coming out of stall #1 (the one who had eaten garlic-smothered Yak the night before). No more stifled laughter behind stall doors, due to the gassy woman in stall #3. No more examining my feet for a rash. Finally, no more hiking through the fog to the toilet in the morning!

It wasn't long before I reveled in daily showers, make-up, shaved legs, earrings, regular hair appointments, as well as the occasional massage. It was a treat to get up early again without disturbing Howard, who liked to sleep in. I appreciated doors and privacy in a completely new light.

Two weeks after we moved in, we picked up my brother and his wife from the airport in Boston; our first guests in what would be a long line of visitors. We had company! I loved cooking with a full-size gas stove on days when the men were too comfy to get up to barbeque. We drank Cape Codders on the deck (they're called Sea Breezes on the west coast) and admired the sunset over the treetops, or listened to rain in the middle of the night and awoke to a freshly scrubbed morning. We went on day trips to Martha's Vineyard, Provincetown, and many points in between. We spent most of our time drinking wine, laughing, and reminiscing. Each month, more company followed, including friends, colleagues from our old careers, and most of our immediate family.

In between guests, I longed to be involved in projects again. I bought a box of oil paints and a few canvasses, took a drawing class, looked for a class on how to refinish furniture, and joined an amazing women's writing group at the Cotuit Center for the Arts. For the next eight months, I would write, read, go thrift store treasure-hunting, make friends with the neighbors, ride bikes with my husband, and spend lots of time alone walking through the woods or taking pictures of the water. I kept the bird feeder full and had to buy a second one to accommodate the noisy Blue Jays. I loved watching them in the morning, cup of coffee in hand, and gasped when I saw my first deep red Cardinal with its black mask. I would throw peanuts onto the back deck for the squirrels and crows, which thrilled Emmy to no end. We even had a regular squirrel that we named Walter, who was fearless, and would stare at Emmy from the other side of the sliding glass door.

Emmy loved everything about Cape Cod.

Howard and I explored Nantucket on bicycles, and stood next to Vice President Joe Biden at a tree lighting ceremony just before Christmas. We visited the John F. Kennedy museum in Hyannis, as well as his library in Boston. In fact, we visited Boston often, walking the Freedom Trail several times; visiting botanical gardens and museums, including my favorite—the beautiful Isabella Gardner Museum, filled with haunting artwork and styled after a Venetian Palazzo. We ate hot dogs at Fenway Park and celebrated my 60th birthday with the Boston Pops in Symphony Hall.

That fall, we took walks on the Harvard campus with Emmy, who saw so many squirrels on the quad that she couldn't decide which one to chase first. Just before Thanksgiving, my awareness shifted while visiting Plymouth to see the Plymouth Rock, when I discovered a plaque explaining how the Wampanoag people were impacted by the white man's invasion. For them, Thanksgiving is a day of mourning, rather than celebration.

When we weren't exploring surrounding areas, we were busy exploring the National Seashore of Cape Cod, or going out for dinner in Mashpee Commons, an upscale outdoor shopping area designed to look like a New England town center. When Lyndsay and Jeff came for a visit, Howard and Jeff disappeared with their clam rakes for several hours on a chilly morning, and came home with a dozen fresh clams straight out of the bay, as well as frozen feet, which they could no longer feel. We were stranded without electricity during several blizzards, but were luckier than most. Then Hurricane Sandy came through, and the Boston Marathon bombing.

I didn't know any of that the day that we signed the lease. I only knew that I wanted to live my life differently, to work harder on my marriage, and to stop ruminating about the past or worrying about the future. I knew it was possible to be happy in my skin again; I didn't have to be perfect, but I did have to get up every morning and try to be a better person. I would stop searching the pockets of those around me for my happiness.

And although I would always want that long look exchanged across a crowded room, I would try not to take it personally if Howard's eye caught the game on TV instead. I would cut him more slack.

On the day that we signed the lease for our new home on the Cape, I didn't think about what would happen next because I finally knew—deep down—that I would always be okay no matter what. That certainty made living in the moment both possible and peaceful.

I also knew that, in spite of everything, neither of us wanted to give up on our marriage. We had the rest of the fall, winter, and spring to heal. We would figure it out.

EPILOGUE

I just got back from a long walk on the Monterey Coastal Recreation Trail, with stunning views of the water at every turn.

We originally rented a small 1-bedroom, 1-bathroom, 714 square foot cottage on the Monterey Peninsula, to see if California was still a good fit for us. It was. A year later, my dream came true: we bought a house in Pacific Grove within walking distance of the ocean.

It didn't take long to join a book club and make new friends. I love my volunteer work as a Guide at the Monterey Bay Aquarium. There are tons of wineries here and I considered getting a part-time job in one of the tasting rooms, but decided (for now) that it would cut into my goal of writing this memoir, reading across a wide swath of genres, volunteering, walking on the beach, taking long bike rides, and spending time with my daughter. Besides, I liked myself better on less wine, not more.

Lyndsay and Jeff got married. They live in Sacramento, about three hours from us. I thought I couldn't be any happier, until they announced a baby was on the way. I am over the moon about becoming an Oma! (Update: Little Aubrey was born in April 2015). Both of my brother's daughters had babies this year—I wish my parents were still alive to see their great-grandchildren. Matt and Maria, and granddaughters Nicole and Madison, live about 4 hours away; son Mike is closer to 5 hours—all within a day's drive. Nicole married her high school sweetheart. Danielle and Brett are still in Austin but came out for a visit to celebrate granddaughter Parker's second birthday.

Howard likes to read, hike, ride his bike, go to the gym every day, and sometimes plays in a poker tournament. He also volunteered to be a scorer for a professional golf tournament. We made new friends at the appreciation dinner that night and came home with several cases of nutrition bars, courtesy of the tournament sponsor. We bought bikes and take the coastal trail as far as we can, before limping back home again (I speak for myself). One of these days we will make it from Pacific Grove to Pebble Beach (10 minutes in the car—at least an hour on a hilly, winding, path by bike). On most mornings, I walk to the Monterey Bay Aquarium and back—4 miles, round trip—and let the ocean soothe my soul instead of vodka.

It's usually sunny, but when it's not, the fog burns off around 11:00 and returns an hour before dark. Every day begins and ends with gratitude. We like to shop and have dinner in the Pacific Grove Village, or head to downtown Monterey to the Osio Theater, a great independent movie theater with a generous senior discount policy.

The house still feels empty after the sudden death of Emily, or beloved traveling companion and family member. She had an entire month of running freely on the beach in Carmel and almost made it to her 13th birthday before her poor heart gave out. I am crying as I write this.

I struggle to describe the impact of my time on Cape Cod. Remember how I joined a writer's group during our first week on the Cape? I often think about the incredible women who quickly adopted me as part of their tribe. We would meet early on Saturday mornings and take turns sharing our work. I was blown away by their talent from the very first class, and even more impressed by their generosity. They took this broken spirit into their hearts and invited me along on cold walks on windy beaches, as well as into their warm kitchens for wine while dinner simmered. They flirted with my husband and laughed at my jokes. I heard poetry in their secrets. I didn't have to be anyone other than who I was.

They taught me to accept myself without reservation or over-analysis. They helped me learn to embrace vulnerability. They celebrated loudly and often. They even threw us a huge good-bye party before we left (the last of *that* hangover is still making its way out of my left eyebrow).

God, I love those women.

Why did we leave? Because our adult children, brother, sisters, and grandchildren were too far away.

I was heartbroken, until I realized that we would somehow find our way back—perhaps as a bi-coastal couple. Cape Cod and I are not through yet; I believe we will have a second home there someday.

So here I sit, in my dream home near the sea, with the man who hung the moon. It's still hard sometimes—you can't put two strong-willed people together and not have friction—but I'm choosing my battles more carefully these days, and so is he. I only have another thirty or so more years on this earth and I am not going to waste time trying to control the future or beat myself up over the past.

When people asked me what I learned during our big adventure, I usually smile and wonder how much to disclose. But since you've come this far with me, I'll share it with you.

I learned that what I thought defined me was false.

I learned that I am still a destination kind of person; living a life of integrity is my new destination.

I learned to recognize when fear is keeping me from doing what I really want to do. Fear of failure, fear of rejection, or fear of looking foolish, is no longer enough to stop me.

I learned that resilience is a muscle that needs to be flexed on a regular basis.

I learned that my chronic bladder infections were really kidney stones!

I learned that my home is finally in my heart, where it belongs.

Finally, I learned that you never know what you might stumble upon if you take the long way home.

Our big adventure accelerated our marriage by at least ten years. Would I do it again? Maybe, under different circumstances, but would I take it all back if I could?

Never.